Writing Sound

An Anthology of Poems by Poets
of the Southern San Joaquin Valley

In collaboration with
The Walter Stiern Library
at California State University, Bakersfield

2019

Many thanks to Dean Curt Asher at the Walter Stiern Library for his ongoing enthusiasm and support of the written word.

Previous issues of the "Writing" series can be found in the Walter Stiern Library Collection at California State University, Bakersfield.

Writing Flora, Writing Fauna (2018)
Writing Work (2017)
Writing the Drought (2016)

Edited by Matthew Woodman

Cover image by Austin Yi

Internal Artwork by Valeria Espinoza

Welcome

What defines the Bakersfield sound? Is it the absence of sweeteners, those strings that render sentiment into syrup? Is it the "do you take this calloused hand in marriage" of Western swing and barroom floor?

On a still day, one can become attuned to the rhythms of the pumpjacks creaking beside the tires on the 99, over the steel wheels on the tracks of the Union Pacific.

Every speaker needs a receiver.

Does the neighbor's barking dog exist if someone doesn't shout "Enough"? Is it really spring if no feline caterwauls spill into the night?

The face speaks into (the phone in) the palm.

[Airplane flies low overhead.]

Does the song expire?

These poems are meant to be read aloud, in coffee shops, waiting rooms, your most comfortable reading chairs. Go ahead, clear your throat. Are you ready now? Good. Let's hear it, then.

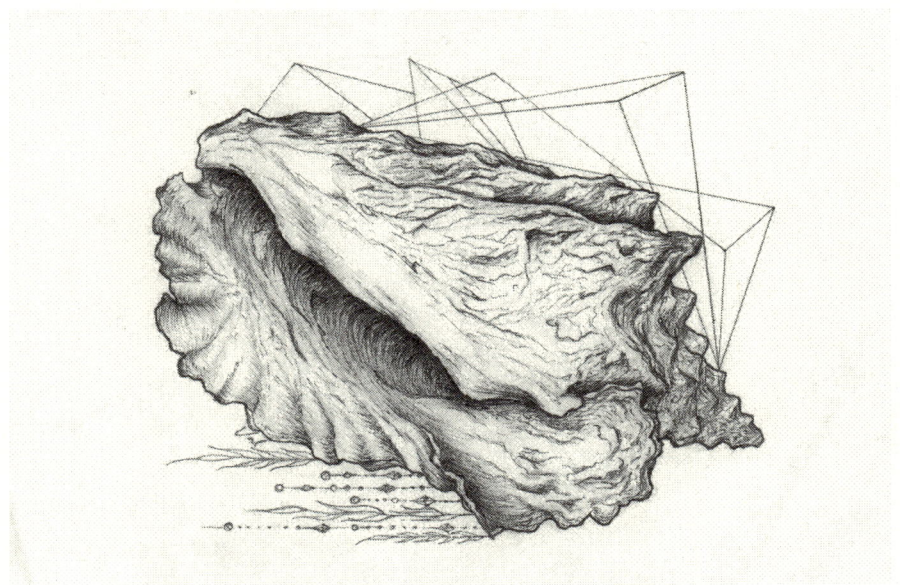

Contents

Katie Gonzalez	"Together"
Jason Grist	"To Measure the Universe" "That Makes Me Want to Write Poetry"
Jack Hernandez	"The Stranger" "Waiting"
Monica Hinson	"Peculiar"
Anke Hodenpijl	"tinnitus" "Our Undersong"
Catherine Abbey Hodges	"Song of the Hinge"
Anthony Salvador Jauregui III	"Line at Marshall's"
Kelsie Nicole Jones	"The Hummingbird's Flight"
Quinn Kelly	"Language" "The Sounds of Mother Nature"
David Kettler	"Mama's Music" "Granite Mind"
Judy Kukuruza	"Sounds Allowed" "Sounds Invited"
Mateo Lara	"Denouement for Silence" "Galore"
Rose Lester	"Authentic Voice" "Starts and Stops"
Diane Lobre	"In Forest Deep" "Ocean Blue"
Vashti Lopez	"G(r)o(w)ing Up" "Iridescent"
Marit MacArthur	"Stealth"
Carla Martin	"The Sound of Creation" "To Bring One Home"
Jerry D. Mathes II	"When My Mother Calls" "What's There"

Audra Miller	"The Sound of Silence"
Mariah Morrow	"Shackled to Mistakes Made Again"
Samantha Nichols	"Mission Moment"
	"Heels"
Christopher Nielsen	"Sounding"
	"Accordion and Fiddle"
Chyna J. Parker	"Mama"
Marc Perez	"Passerby of a Barking Rottweiler"
	"Turn the Key"
Shelby Pinkham	"Mixtape for Mourning"
Nashwa Rafiq	"Too One Tea One"
Diana Ramirez	"Left Unsaid/Muffled"
	"Verbalize/Vocalize"
Michael Repik	"Open Mic"
	"I, Silence"
Bailey Russell	"The Silence is Deafening"
	"Speaking with No Voice"
Caroline Russell	"Boom!"
	"Music, Melodious Secrets"
Sidney Russell	"Gold Is Rare"
	"The Voice"
Jennifer Samano	"Broken"
B. Jordan Schmoll	"Mphondorho, a lion spirit"
	"Sounds of Home"
Sa'miah Shakir	"Up the Stairway"
	"To Know Knowledge"
Myles C. Shell	"The Sea-Scape"
Lena Smallwood	"The Sound"

Don Thompson	"Coming and going" "Along the slough"
Donna Valdivia	"Detention Room" "House Party Aftermath"
Fernando Valdivia	"Café Symphony" "Lake Huron"
Dylan Vaughn	"May"
Tim Vivian	"The Language of Mosquitoes" "Your Forgiveness: During the Final Days of Masada Peter Speaks"
Michelle Whitaker	"Whispering"
Jana Lee Wong	"Thunder" "Sounds of the Dust Bowl"
Matthew Woodman	"A Mean Piece of Water" "The Fugitive"
Austin Yi	"Effervescent" "Jungles in the Dead of Night"

Rhymes Like Knives

Oh, the horror of this unsheathing sound!
The noise you hear before your body hits the ground.
Where you're surrounded in liquid that tastes of metal,
With the environmental sound around you that hasn't settled.
The sound of arteries tearing as your ears ring,
And yet, even with a gruesome event,
Someone sings.
Shing, shing, shing!
Goes the knife, handle attached to a wrist with a powerful cling.
The sound of your heartbeat alongside the interruption of bloodstream,
Makes one hell of a product for a deafening scream.

--Sarah Alnagar

Boil, Bubble

in which we revel in endless dream
welcoming matters of attachment
a body becomes conduit &
wouldn't you think these
parasitic tendencies would
hi-jacking silently cell
by cell, look come stare
inside needle-hole pricking
best intentions, set a wave
of water, heat on high
this is what we were meant
for impulse inferno
watch water ripple
like us in hot pursuit
playing games holding
our breath for a moka pot
boiling eggs, bubble up
steam-over, a porcelain
beauty, unsuspecting of
anything here in the hand
holding my breath, harmless
suffocating of any darkness in
a battered world one motion
becomes another becomes
our spurting effort darker
than coffee, a moka pot
churning, boiling our magic
destroying & dissolving worry.

--Shawn Anto

Cradle

close your eyes   take a deep breath   what do you see?

    a tree sapling   sweating blood   leaves dissolving   standing

humanoid silhouette   pulsating heart   head pooling   drenching

    blood   at its feet.

good let's start your run here.

close your eyes   take a deep breath   what do you see?

my mother standing in front of the bedroom
                          she is holding a hand out to   *him*
my mother is standing in front of the bedroom
                          she's crying   *she's apologizing*

it	*was*	*just*	*that*	*one*	*time.*		
good.		*run*	*with*	*that.*			
good.		*build*	*your*	*pace*	*with*	*that.*	

a steady rhythm pulsing as I reorganize memories, cluttered tomb in a manner of fluttering, in a matter of neutrality charging, until the next trigger starts appearing, another beat-beat, tap-tap on a temple in the hollowness of this cavity.

--Shawn Anto

Strangers in a Coffee Shop

They meet again
Or is it the first time?

Electric static fills the room

They sip coffee between special words
Words that will be muttered later to each other again
They cling to each word as if it were a gift

Words spoken sweet
Words spoken carefully
They can't get enough of the words

She looks down with a crooked smile
He gazes deep
She can feel him

They finish their coffee
A napkin folds

--Sherean Bledsoe

A Musical Cento

Will I ever make a sound?
Take a breath and look around...
Walk right by and never even know I'm there,
In the velvet darkness;
Floating, falling sweet intoxication
Agony, misery, woe
Is this home?

Silently the senses abandon their defenses,
Caught in a celluloid jam.

Purge your thoughts of the life you knew before,
There's a light...
Do you wanna ride?
My heart's far, far away
So before I lead with the worst of me,
Hear these words and have faith,
I have been changed for good!

Another day, another destiny
I can hear the bells,
I'll be astonishing!
One last time:
I wanna do more than survive.

I hope I haven't taken too much of your time.

--Greg C. Bolanos

Hello, Darkness

Inhale.

Death is my captive
Imprisoned in all chambers
My heart delivers daily beatings;
It breaks free with each breath
Love labors fruitlessly, inevitably
It escapes again.
Claiming a birth right of sound
Bound for infinity
Crossing stars to lovers indiscriminately-

Exhale.

The jail bird will sing
Endless songs
In my lifetime,
But only once will it sing for me.
Then, only then, will I
Hum along
To the song

Of silence.

--Greg C. Bolanos

Nature Journal: Entry No. 12

A Coal Mine is Devouring a 12,000 Year Old Forest
—'Bloomberg' 3 Dec. 2018

*We multiplied and fought and gobbled until there was nothing left, and then we died....we did
not adapt. We destroyed ourselves. But we destroyed the world first.*
— Ursula K. Le Guin

It looks like a buzz saw the size of a three story building trenching
through twelve thousand years of sylvan ecosystem at the echoed pace
of an anti-primordial-belch the length of half a time-and-a-half workday.
It glazes with saw-debris, dust and twenty pound shards of wood—a mulch lot.

It's common to cut at the iniquities of one self. At lunch though, it will go nearly
silent like an abandoned shopping mall, lauded within by the resonance of its own
emptiness and a distant intrepid cacophony. Workers eat sandwiches there where
the food court will have been, while suits at a modular table two nations and a sea

away, break for lièvre à la royale with a portion of steamed chopped vegetables—
mixed broccollini, cauliflower branches, baby buttery carrots carved into florets
no larger than a dozen neo-fetal pipistrelles, all deliberately placed haphazard
on the plate, because we eat with our eyes that gluttonously too if its allowed.

Yet why have to recklessly gorge on all we see? That less-easier swallowed
hope that we become hungrier for lasting nourishment, should not subside.

--Jeremy Casabella

Dead Ringers

The vinyl sky anticipates
resonant diatonics.

Every coffin's
coffin bell could

be an angel, cherub
or seraphim,

awakened in its cell—
an unbroken Schrodinger's

utterance ringing-in
its stillness with blaring synchrony.

--Jeremy Casabella

Double Dutch

Thunk, thunk, swoosh

Down in the Valley
Where the green grass grows

Thunk, thunk, swoosh

There sat Sally
Sweet as a rose

Thunk, thunk, swoosh

If I had a nickel
For every time Sally
Sat in the Valley

Thunk, thunk, swoosh

And we kids skipped
Sweet as a rose
'Tween the double ropes

Thunk, thunk, swoosh

Bounced, swerved
Zig-zagged
Left and right

Thunk, thunk, swoosh

The cadence
Our heart beats
Filling the air

Thunk, thunk, swoosh

If I had a nickel
I'd be yours
'Til soda pops

--Annis Cassells (First published in *You Can't Have It All,* March 2019)

Life Out Loud

The world roared to life
With the gentle placement
Of the long-sought aids
Tawny plastic curved
Behind his freckled ears
The world became a lion

Overwhelming
      Over-the-top
            Overpowering

He'd never heard, never known
Chairs scuffed floors
Flatware clattered on plates
Book pages rustled when flicked
Lips smacked during dinner
Brillo pads screeched on pots and pans

His neck muscles twitched and tensed
With the sizzle of bacon
Plunk of typewriter keys
Squeak of rocking chairs
Blast of car horns in rush hour

Until, teeth clenched,
He couldn't take it any more
Tore loose those offending aids
And like a lucky crapshooter
Tossed them into a drawer,
Shut off life's loudness

--Annis Cassells

(First published in *You Can't Have It All,* March 2019)

Sound Paradigm: 2 a.m.

I made a mistake
rain drop ripples-drip
freeway cars:
1, 2, 3, drip
4, drip
5, 6, 7, drip drip

I made many mistakes
toss left-creak
toss right-creak
on my belly-creak
on my back-creak
old fucking bed springs

No, you're a mistake
bed sheets rustling
congested chest whimpering
nostril breath biting
blinking eyes shuttering-drip

No, I made a mistake
Clock-tic drip tic drip tic drip tic drip
every second, every ripple
8, 9, drip drip
toss left
toss right
belly
back

drip

Maybe, I'm the mistake

--Carla Chacon

Apoptosis

until I swallow every vocal cord,
until these fingernails peel this
fraudulent flesh against the dirt,
until this abdomen bursts,
until I'm stripped naked,
unembellished to the soul:

I want to screech!

Condemn and curse
these sins away,
until each etches a final, frantic
memory into the lining of my trachea,
until exorcised into the atmosphere
for someone else to inhale.

--Carla Chacon

The Last Show

Buck Owens had finished
the first half of the show
at his Crystal Palace
in Bakersfield.

He stood silently
in the dark corridor
surrounded by fans,
and no one spoke to him.

He seemed to stare at me,
recognizing one of
two ladies that revived
a man whose heart had stopped
and fell during his show
a few years back.

Although he was tired,
Buck gave the songs his best shot
for his fans who had driven
all the way from Oregon.

After the performance,
later that night,
Buck died in his sleep.

But he lives on in his songs:
"I came here in looking for somethin'
I couldn't find anywhere else . . . .
Trying to find me something better
On the streets of Bakersfield."

--Portia Choi

Meditation Bowl

A hand holds a stick that strikes a brass bowl.
A resounding clang reverberates in the bowl--
the vibrations become softer, softer and
softer into silence.

The mind becomes still: breathing slowly, in and out.
        Within a few minutes, the cleared mind becomes muddled
        with worryworryworry--
details of all the things to do, today.

With continued slow, deep breaths: in…out…in…out;
        the lips mouth the same word, over and over: Om. . Om;
        a glow gently appears in the mind of the meditator.

Breathing in and out.
A submerged emotion swells out.
Each breath, a courage to be aware of the feeling
and allow the
tears to stream down the face and
to drip from chin to lap.
An awareness—ah, this emotion is still here,
to be released again.

Breathing in and out.
Sight-sense becomes intense.
Incense smoke drifts upward circling around the
curved petals of a blue iris.
Morning sunlight surrounds the meditator,
casting a shadow on the wall.

Bowl is struck, the ringing wakens the mind to its surroundings.

And I am transformed, awakened to live more fully—
to listen more, understand more,
breathe slowly more.

--Portia Choi

Ukulele Princess

ukulele princess, play to the tune
of sleepless nights, of the waning moon
of light, of afterlife, of a fresh start
of healing light over dark hearts

ukulele princess, use your fingers
speak in chords and let them linger
hide in the notes, dream for refrain
pull the nylon, pick my brain

my ukulele princess plays me like the strings
of her wooden beauty, but at least she sings
to the melody of my heart being plucked from my chest
as long as she plays, I'll never get any rest

--Taylor Clark

Hummingbirds Never Know the Words

Hummingbirds
Never know the words
Because they're in too big a hurry
To ever stop and worry.
They move on to the next flower and
If the nectar isn't sour
Then they will take a sip . . . .

"Hmmmmmmm," hummed the hummingbird. "Tra la la,
hmmmmmmmmmmmmmmmmmmmmmmmmmmmmmmmmmmmmmmmmmmmm
mmmmm?

One flower down, only nine hundred ninety-nine to go--
Not that I'm counting, but scientists, ornithologists,
I am told--with their slide-rules and microscopes,
And their probes, have clocked us at a rate of a
Thousand flowers per diem, which is the fancy-pants
Scientists' way of saying per day. In Latin, no less,
Only used now in surgical--or situations liturgical,
Or when naming the flora and fauna, by genus and species,
Like calling me *Calliphlox amethystina* 'stead of plain old
Amethyst Woodstar, or *Metallura phoebe* for Black Metaltail.
Heliothryx aurita for Black-eared Fairy;
Lesbia victoriae for Black-tailed Trainbearer;
Trochilus scitulus for Black-billed Streamertail!

One thousand per day! 'Hmmmmm,' the scientists say.
'That's a lot of nectar.'

A heck of a lot of nectar. Hmmmmmmmmmmmm, and tra la la la.
But it takes a heck of a lot of nectar to fuel this plane.
I never stop to count the flowers. Hmmmmmm?
I guess you could say, 'I wing it.'

While wending my way through the warp and woof of time,
Weaving my way through the warp and the weft,
Why worry about words and whether they rhyme?
Why wonder what word best describes my emotion?
When what really matters is: my wings are in motion.

The tortoise, porcupine, or possibly opossum,

Move at a pace where such notions may blossom.
Maybe a mirror in a palace of perfection
Could afford the luxury to support such idle reflection?

I have not the time, as I hover in space.
Look how fast I have to flap my wings
To remain in the air,
Suspended in one place?"

Hummingbirds
Never know the words
Because they're in too big a hurry
To ever learn the lyrics--
Discuss philosophy with clerics
In the middle of a circus.
No, they'll leave that to the poets.
Words are all they have to work with.

-- Christopher Robert Craddock

Pat Martino had a stroke
E A D G B

Up until then he'd been a moderately successful Jazz Guitarist
But he awoke from the stroke to discover that he could no longer play guitar.
It was the reversal of the joke where the man awoke from anesthesia.
The doctor assured him the operation had been a complete success.
He'd be back to normal in no time.

"But will I be able to play the piano?" he enquired.

"I don't see any reason why not," said the Physician.

"That's funny . . . because I couldn't play it before."

Pat Martino had a stroke
E A D G B

So, anyway, though Pat Martino had completely forgotten how to play the
        guitar,
He taught himself how to play again--from scratch.
Not only that, his beginner's mind gave him a fresh perspective.
He began to see music in terms of geometric shapes that had hitherto been
        hidden.
The 'scales' fell from his eyes. He saw Diminished chords as squares.
Augmented chords formed isosceles triangles.
Minor Seventh chords were trapezoids.

Pat Martino had a stroke
E A D G B

"How did all that mathematical mumbo jumbo
Help his music?" I can hear the skeptics among you grumbling.
Well, he was able to navigate treacherous chord changes
Avoiding the point of diminishing returns and any trapezoids
That might have snared him.

Sometimes the crack
Lets in the light.

Pat Martino had a stroke
E A D G B

It was a stroke of luck, a stroke of genius.
It was the fabled different stroke since he'd awoke a different folk.
Sometimes the breast stroke is not the best stroke,
And an isosceles triangle can be the best augmentation of all.

[The Poet takes out an·orchestral triangle and strikes it thusly]

Ting.

-- Christopher Robert Craddock

Rumble

The low roar of my 4Runner
warming up. I never saw
it new, and it never did
sound the same after
the driveline and bad U-joints
incident.

The barrage of my alarm tone is
always startling and
palpitation-inducing,
not at all a rumble— in effect,
only noise.

The rumble, but NOT
Let's Get Ready To Rumble.
I'm not a fan of
Micael Buffer on the mike or
the ring of painful
thuds and thumps.

The embarrassing gurgle of
my stomach that precedes
my hangry — fair warning
those Snickers commercials
weren't lying.

The unmistakable vibration
of my belly laugh
as a kid blows a
loud, wet raspberry
on my cheek.

A snapshot of time,
told through the senses,
Just another short
story for the ears.

--Nilsa Cubiascanas

2 lives- One Book

I flipped *absent-mindedly* through our pages of life

--fingertips grazing, barely
feeling, or giving
presence in the lives of other's

But

She turned them slowly,

she with the breath of life,
immersed
-touching and feeling every letter,
imprinting ourselves in inked symbols

I ripped through the pages *angrily*

--tearing some apart as unfairness
and terror reigned our life

But

She turned them with *tenderness* and *sadness*

-pasting them back—
hurt
--dripping down her face to stain
the ink, forgiving the toner that
smudged our letters

I flipped them with *hatred*

-every word *screeching* obscenities, *tainted*, and *stained*
by the rewrite of other's

But

She pried them open *lovingly*

-stroking the binding as a smile *danced*
on her lips, finding beauty within every corner of the sheets,
"her reflection smiled so beautifully her dimple deepened
in the mirror's image"

And

She *laughed* and *inhaled* the ink scribed leaves

-her soul *emanating* with warmth and happiness, "her

laugh causing her best friend to smile in response"
But

I *took* a hold of the twined leaves and *shut* them with overwhelming
desperation
        -finality
            ringing
                with
                    Silence

--Yazmin De La Torre

Días de Adopción

The have given the child several names
"ugly, useless, idiot, mute, but no one
remembers the endearment given by the mother.
The six-year-old slumps in a moldy, brown corner,
a loose ragged night gown draping,
the tiny shivering frame underneath,
shuffling across its skin.
"They might come tonight,"
The humanistic doll whispers to itself.

The other children at Saint Maria's Orfanato whisper
secrets of survival tactics for the
visit every third day of the week
that always seemed to take place at midnight.

Diana the cook always sings to herself
as she sends the boys to bed after supper.
She often shuts herself in her room and
the smell of something sweet and flowery
dances just outside her door as she sings off key.

The older children lock their doors before sleep,
but they never say why, their faces weary and drawn.
They won't even look when the mute speaks.
And since the door doesn't have a lock,
the children that share the room try to barricade
the door with an old and rusted metal bed frame.
The older boys that were in the room
take to cowering with dread across the room
their spot under the newspaper cladded window.

The door creaks *open*.

The sun peeks through the cracks of the door,
shadowing the children making them disappear
but it's so bright it hurts the fledgling's eyes causing it to look down
but the sun continues its path and drips something wet
and hot down on the brood's arm
that becomes hard and cracks on the skin with movement.
The other boy's hug each other tighter and look away from the door
tears streaming silently down their soot dusted cheeks.

The child's body reeks of fear.
They have come now.
They are here.

--Yazmin De La Torre

In Memoriam: Mnemosyne

We forget what were mere fantasy
Wherein memory masquerades:
Such are the sounds of the Valley

Of promises, hinging on stolid gazes. We
Fall together, two graceless bodies,
We forget what were mere fantasy.

The draw into an opaque umber galaxy
Awakens exquisite scarlet mushroom clouds.
Such are the sounds of the Valley.

Amid fathomless stacks where idle dreams flee,
Grinding out porcelain and ideas,
We forget what were mere fantasy.

Metabolic gymnastics within a clinging tree
Beside oil pumps' creaking frame Panoramic views.
Such are the sounds of the Valley

That enshroud a busy safety wild emergency,
Where echoes relent and memory betrays.
We forget what were mere fantasy,
Such are the sounds of the Valley.

--Jeff Eagan

Asunder

Dimming is your soul
now that hearts are apart,
leaving humming darkness.
There I woke, reaching under
the faint light of the moon.

Croaks from afar diluted by the chirping crickets
whose existence is heard yet rarely seen,
sounding to guide me away from you.

There will be an ever-sounding darkness
in the absence of your fading light.
It's getting late and you continue escaping,
wounded is your heart.

With the light of the fire fairies gone,
the birds' signing dwindling to nothing
and no more, back to how things started.

Tell me before we are gone, as it once was,
what was and what remains.

Harness the wind
that destroys the remaining crisp leaves
who wait the final fall,
existing until the end of the season,
welcoming the start of mild silence
and cold, white darkness.

Awaiting the silenced fall of flakes
and patters of the rain.
The flowing stream soon to be frozen,
stilled by the change until it lives once more.

There will be silent darkness again.
Let the awful song be heard
but remember me when we are nothing and no more.

--Valeria Espinoza

The Sounds of Youth

Out, crying
One of just two buzzes I knew to say

Loud, laughing
The better of both to come out my mouth;

I didn't know to say anything else.

"Sleep, child
For your rest is of the most important"

"Drink, gulp, breathe
Commit to your body's evolution;"

These were the foundations of how I lived.

You hear me,
Not I you, and you become my life guide.

You know me,
Not I you, but I learn how you live.

I listen to what you tell me to know.

Laugh, cry, grow
A simple life with you I grew to know.

When you became them, there was much more noise.

Suddenly, more regulations echoed;

I then didn't know what to listen to.

--Zeltzin Estrada-Rodriguez

Stunted Evolution by the Deafening Box

Can't you hear me screaming?

Before, nearly always, you would read my mind
Now, inside
A soundproof room of glass
You are my mind.

My roars, my bellows
My cries,
Muffled and dampened
Into eventual repercussions of nothingness.

I lost my sound in this box.
As the orders piled on,
The lines became more concise and narrow,
My resounding colors turned mute.

Eyes closed,
You're all that I hear.
Eyes open,
Your vibrations linger stronger in the air.

Can't you hear me screaming?

Surrounded by one-way mirrors,
My mouth goes unseen.
Soundproofed in,
My screams go unheard.

I used to sit, fastened in a chair
Watching everything you did
Hearing everything you said
Until I realized the locks could be broken by my hands.

No longer sitting, now I pace,
Searching for doors out of this box,
Listening for sounds, looking for sights
Unowned by you.

Howling, wailing,
Hollering out

You look toward my box
And smile at the reflecting sight of you.

Can't you hear me screaming?

Tired of following your every move,
Though they founded pieces of my soundness,
I long for my uniquely loud whole;
No longer can I stand unheard to dead kings and queens.

Grabbing the legs of the broken chair,
I swing towards the walls
The glass crackles,
The smallest of cracks creep.

Every day I swing,
I bang
My arms growing stronger with the practice,
The walls cracking crevices grow deeper.

Alas, the final thundering thud
The glittering image of you shattered
And screeched against the newly found,
Unbounded floor.

I scream, and you turn around.
I scream, and we hear foundations mounted by you,
but resounding freedom found by a finally evolving me.

--Zeltzin Estrada-Rodriguez

Random Sounds

Random sounds I enjoy the most:
    Raindrops tapping,
    Softly rapping
On the tin roof at the coast;

From the window late at night,
    I hear commotion
    Of the ocean
Waving wildly in moonlight;

Surf crashing in the sand,
    Loudly pounding
    Then resounding,
Smashing, bashing again and again;

Dog's nails click on the wood floor
    As she's running,
    Sounds so funny,
Makes me laugh out loud some more!
(At thirteen, she usually walks around
Aimlessly wandering – she's a hound!);

The sweet chirp of birds in spring,
    Calling out
    With a shout.
I love to hear whatever songs they sing;

Sometimes it's completely quiet,
    My stomach will growl,
    I want to howl!
(It is my gut, I can't deny it;
I think it's hysterical, a riot!);

At family gatherings to hear
    Giggles of a child
    Makes me smile,
It is like music to my ear;

The songs of Billy Joel, Adele,
      Three Dog Night,
      Barry White,
Soothe my soul till I feel well;

Hearing someone call my name
      Lovingly
      Assures me
Everything will be okay.

These are some of the sounds that play
Between my ears, day by day.

--Shelley J. Evans

The Sounds of Silence

The sounds of silence
(I don't hear them)
that's the point
the quiet is sublime

I'll take it any time

No yelling, no barking
of dogs down the street
no car horns honking
THIS IS SWEET

Tranquility cannot be beat

Noise-free and peaceful
my favorite zone
I even silenced
my iPhone

No more incessant ring tone

I wonder how long I have
to enjoy this respite
with sounds of silence filling
my ears tonight

In the calm quietude I write

--Shelley J. Evans

Rat-a-tat tat!

4:35 am! Rat-a-tat. It's time to get up!
Aww, I hit the snooze Nine more minutes please…
Rat-a-tat-TAT-TAT! OK I'm up!
To the beat I march semi- soldier like,
but there are no drill sergeants in sight
To work I go to cook and clean
At home I return do the same and do the same for me
My day unfolds the humming of a low staccato
No real rush now just a slow and steady outflow

Noontime arrives and with it the snares crescendo
A bright clattering of beats moves me to dance
I move back and forth as if in a trance
like a marching band of one,
a lone woman show.
Out the door and in my car I go
I rush to class that starts at 1!
As I drive my speakers blow
the beginning of
Eryka's 'window seat' a hiphop flow
Rat a tat tat-tat, tat- tat ta-tat
The initial drumbeat pulls out in front
To lead the beats along
Paired with strings getting plucked
And winded toots of the brass
My day is winding down to dusk
The evening breaks
the drum decrescendoes
quieter and quieter still until to bed I go
The day ends with a fading pitch beat
silence comes over me as I fall asleep
in my bed poised to awaken and repeat.

--Vickie Gage

Five-Part Harmony

Enticed!

she serenades with her approaching waves that mimic
the hem of her dress and the curling of her finger
sings sweetly her song in falsetto and at once
you react with movement from your legs to meet her

Ecstatic!

she recedes in hums and lifts her skirts for a brief moment
whispers "come closer" to hear her open-mouthed melody
charms again by the crashing chaos of her rhythms
percussion at the thumping of your feet grows steady

Enamored!

her waltz with the moon dazzles and swoons that of
the hardest man to envious clay (hint at the Red Sea)
until you demand to steal her thunderous kiss
harmony in your greedy eyes growl "mine" and plunge

Engulfed!

her sensational caress sends shivers down your spine
strikes and swallows you whole as your trembling teeth
bring back the castanets of May when suddenly
you remember that feeling of being alive before the

End!

--Karissa Garcia

Together

pristine instruments clink
to signal delicate tranquility

chaos of kinetic energy
thrown from the wind
into the pendulous pipes

within the hollow vessel,
a ladybug seeks shelter
from the great-tailed grackle
that looms in waiting

a spirit's way to leave
a final echo in our world
before it passes on

evidence that the wind picks up
and through the metal pipes
it breaks apart

memory of a family
and like the wind,
breaks apart

--Katie Gonzalez

To Measure the Universe

With the first hint
Of dawn
I grab my pen
And set out
To write the universe
Between the first silhouette
Of mountains
And the sound
Of a rooster.

--Jason Grist

That Makes Me Want to Write Poetry

It's the sound leaves make
Rolling over the ground
And rolling over one another
That makes me want
To write poetry,
The wind that shakes acid
From an orange tree,
A mountain
Providing shade and light
Having wrinkled its brow
Squinting to see the sun

--Jason Grist

The Stranger

The stranger is always among us
sitting alone at a small table
hands embracing a frothed coffee,
standing in a crowd
moving swirling
like a flock of birds
strutting on a decorated street,
The stranger among us
may someday be us
waiting in fettered loneliness
for a voice to free our hearts.

--Jack Hernandez

Waiting

He sat on a rock
waiting for waters
to part   impatience
kept his gaze
on the silent sea

Seasons passed
as his hair thinned
into white strands

He ignored the waves
chanting at his feet.

--Jack Hernandez

Peculiar

Hushed cozy twilight,
        Lulling melody of tranquility.
Coffin encapsulated by warmth.
        Slumber grazes her eyelids;
Dreams peep around the corner.
                Sudden surge of clamor!
Boisterous barrage begins.
        Adrenaline discharges abruptly.
Foreign explosion perplexing,
        Odd hour, frightening.
                Mystery causes panic.
Too complacent to investigate…

--Monica Hinson

tinnitus

bones that groan

jowls that click, click, click

that yapping little dog next door
that just won't quit

the guy in the booth behind you
as he hawks a huge lugie into his napkin

the death penalty

the argument with mom
when I left home

the promises I make to myself
unspoken, usually put aside

the children's tears
as I fought with their father

the fear, the joy, the courage
when I left

large and small sounds persevere
ringing, ringing, ringing

not all of them require
my attention

--Arke Hodenpijl

Our Undersong

winter's reclusive songbird
cantillates a somber aria
into the murky mist of early morning,
standing on crystal covered branch
she sings her lamentations
as fluttering vapors uncurl from her rostrum,
her uncluttered hymn
hangs in the frigid air
like smoldering smoke from a distant campfire
companionless and isolated

winter's demeanor
demands that the inflection of suffering
drift into the soul
visible only in that solitary moment,
but heard for an eternity.
a melancholy thick
with memories
wanting to be seen
wanting to wait
in the fog
of human compassion.

--Anke Hodenpijl

Song of the Hinge

At Fantastic Sam's some time back,
        sitting in the chair, looking at myself
                looking back from the mirror, my hair falling

                to the shiny floor, for no particular reason
        I can remember I asked the young woman
wielding the scissors what she liked most

about her job. She thought for a moment—
        snip snip—and then said *I love the sound
                of the scissors*. Ever since then, I've thought

                about the sounds of a vocation, wondered
        if love of those could be a kind of measure:
have you found your true work?

Do you love its sounds? Lighthouse keepers,
        your foghorns? Violinists, the snap
                of your case, opening? Jockeys, the stomp

                and nicker? I have no idea what I'm talking about,
        of course, except when I'm speaking of myself,
and then only partially. Speaking of myself,

for myself, I love the scritch scritch
        of a room of students writing. Not typing,
                or keyboarding as we say these days, but pen-

                to-paper, hand-moving-across-the-page writing,
        a sound that I associate with a second sound
as the result of a dream.

In this dream I had a giant
        pad of paper—taller than me—
                and I understood that my task was to write

                in it, fill it up. So I did, filled the first page
        with words from top to bottom, then turned
the page which, in that moment, turned

into a door. If I walked through, I brought
        no memory of that back from the dream,
            but ever since then the textured sound of many

            writers writing makes me think of the sounds
        a door makes as it opens: click of latch, squeak
of hinge. It's 10:30 in the morning,

7:45 in the evening, and we're bent to the page,
        thirty of us, filling it up, writing our doors. I have
            no idea—and I mean none—what their doors

        will open on, or mine for that matter,
            when the latch clicks, when the hinge
                sings its small song.

--Catherine Abbey Hodges

Line at Marshall's

For C.D'A, M.A., & S.A

A pair of pizza socks
soaks up the sweat in
my right palm, I'm nervous
but it's not my first rodeo—
I'm no virgin—
I've been to a Ross before.

Marshalls was just a competitor—
a challenger—
a first cousin.

The line's forward progress grows as quickly
as soup day at a homeless shelter—
broccoli cheddar day— a complete surprise to me.
*Cheddar contains lactose and roughly 65% of the
world is intolerant towards lactose type products*
I suppose living on the street has its advantages.

(UN)fortunately I had a home. One that
moaned and croaked and bellowed out screams
the way an ant does when you burn it alive
after twisting its little ant antennae until he says
"daddy."

Thought after thought encapsulates
all the empty spaces in my mind
capable of holding any random vibration
that comes in contact with a smidgen of air.
Air that will escape my ear
the same way a turkey baster
sucks air any time it's used in an
open setting or non-human orifice.

A pat on my right overweight shoulder
reverberates as far as it possibly can—
enough to startle me and simultaneously knock out
a single Airpod from the clutches of my left ear
named Oswaldo.

"F**k the Pain Away by Peaches" pauses—

"I can help the next person on number 6"

--Anthony Salvador Jauregui III

The Hummingbird's Flight

A flickering light caresses the dark
A trickle of warmth slowly creeps in,
Unnoticed by the cacophony of chaos
It slowly envelops the cold blackness
Embracing the frozen center until it melts
Revealing a tiny and desperate hummingbird
Fluttering frantically, frightened and hungry
Completely blind, she's drawn to the warm light
There's something there, she nervously flies around it, curious,
Until finally landing on an exquisite flower
An intricate rose with delicate petals of deep red
Practically glowing in the dim candlelight
The rose, bursting with nectar, remains still
The nervous hummingbird begins to calm
Drinking sweet nectar, relaxing with every sip
The light grows, slowly revealing a painting of colors
She finally flutters away, full of renewed vitality
Into a world of bright colors and a calming warmth

-- Kelsie Nicole Jones

Language

Sound. Speech.
Tongues flapping.
Uvulas pulsating.
Lapping of saliva.

A baby's cry.
Tongues in rhythm,
tongues in romance.
An old man's breath,
a husband's last dance.

Speech. Sound.
People talk,
real talk,
cattle, walk.
Rhythm in flux. A hundred ways to speak.

Speech; consonants, rhythm, vowels. All of these things. To speak, to be.
Speak, spoke.
Spoken.

--Quinn Kelly

The Sounds of Mother Nature

The coo of a cockatiel, placent on its branch.
The wood creaks. A fluttering of wings. Its
lone bristles causes the plants of stir.

The tree comes down with a crash. It splints.

Frigid boxes with no sound,
ice come crashing down.

The low hum-drum of a bus refusing to move.
Rushing wind, besides my face. A low, stubborn
vibration from the earth. The wind gives
a cackle. Me thinks doth protest too much.

The waves crash against the beach and shlick
the sand into mud. 19 dead, freak tsunami to
blame. Tragedy. The clickety-clack of small
hands against a glass screen.

Tap, tap.

Hole in one. A protest, a mockery. A chant from
his people's people. They chant back til they
leave with raspy throats, and a silent kricking
of hollow bricks.
21 dead, a school shooting.

--Quinn Kelly

Mama's Music

The music mama played
was the only of its kind
It etched beautiful grooves
in the vinyl of my mind

The organ's tone wheel
mixing up the sound
Took me for a ride
spinning round and round

The Gulbrandsen and its chimes
Played Silent Night to me
Ragtime let me know
There was jazz in our family tree

I hear the sounds today
in modern music played
Whatever the genera,
the memories have stayed

The rhythms in my blood,
the beat within my heart
A familiar sound to me
right from the music's start

The Hammond strikes a chord,
A piano strikes one two
My dear sweet mama's hands…
showed me what to do

--David Kettler

Granite Mind

Voices that etch,
The granite of my mind
Subtle their tone,
my tensions unwind

Melodic harmonies
that often will stay
From the vibrating voice
of one David Gray

Don Henley and drums,
That beat oh so smooth
Adele is pure honey
To calm and to soothe

The rasp of Neil Young's cords
And the truth of Leonard Cohen
Have Conor Oberst...
and the Avett Bros knowin

Marcus Mumford and Sons...
and his Irish convulse
Quicken Jeff Tweedy,
and Mike Rosenberg's pulse

My mind and my heart
and a bit of my soul
can never give back
what the true artist stole

With real emotion
that comes from the gut
impressions are made
from voices that cut

I always can soar
with the wings of my ears
and bathe all my sorrows
in creative tears

The real singer
with fire and with sizzle
Etch in my heart...
with the words like a chisel

--David Kettler

Sounds Allowed

Only in my head,
as I allow...
The caw of the crow—
wind soughing through pliant leaves.

Traffic swooshing, rumbling trains,
voices that grate, chafe—
shrill, raspy, accusatory, whiny,
a cacophony undecipherable...
these are not allowed.

The cry of the lost inland seagull,
my dog's nails on the wood floor...
The gull, my dog,
I allow.

Selective hearing...
sounds I allow.
The quiet voice enters,
"I love you."

Only in my head
as I allow,
oozing into the soul...
bringing peace, calm, unity.
Sounds I allow.

—Judy Kukuruza

Sounds Intuited

"Where are you!"
A desperate small voice
sounding lost,
fearful, panicky.

"I'm fine."
Words lie, sound is honest.
The sound of pain
is louder than the forced words.

"Ask me about my day…"
The smile in the voice,
happy excitement,
bursting to share.

"Yes!"
Triumph, victory.
Sounds of exuberance,
progress ahead.

"How's it going?"
Silence, a nod.
No sound.
Silence of the wounded.

Not the words,
not the facial expressions…
The timbre, the tone.
Sounds beneath the sounds intuited.

—Judy Kukuruza

Denouement for Silence

this is our 'brutal best':
        flinging burning books
        out of windows, rain pours
             and

_____

        butterflies noon our eyes
        wasps evening flesh
            and

_____

        can't cut or stake claim
        where revelations are
        you sucking skin
        brown boy being jewel
        fingers slip into a dream
            and

_____

        storm washes you home
        papa's been gone two years
        a severe rip still resonates here
        in the gut, we can't say, we just feel
            and

_____

        bitterness like soap in our mouths lilting
        acidic juice burning wound   we   came   here
for   answers   that   we   still   wait   for.

--Mateo Lara

Galore

Inspired by the song 'Love Galore' by SZA

[I need

      I need

            I need

                  I need]

come closer & feel wettest ache   slippery sentiment   encroaching on

your display of affection

touch   their names   …   …   …   their deaths

      transgress   temper   fury   fingering   soft

      space   bless

          remember nothing

      caress

              hit you up

      depress

              cause a fall

              [no   no

                  no   no

                      no

  no

  no   no

      no.]

I say farewell

      only if you give me another hour or two

you will refuse a ceremony of trust, misguide us into another harmful place

cannot stay here// cannot live with your noise.

long as we got   what?   reverberate through these streets

claim nothing but   …   their homes   their thrones

    …

    [love

    love

      love.]

listen   to   the   pink-purr

a   whirr   of   abundance.

                  --Mateo Lara

Authentic Voice

Sitting at a picnic table, my reverie is interrupted.
Awakened now, I notice the sound of leaves rustled by the gentle breeze.
The pages of my journal shudder in response.
Crows caw and sparrows chirp in the branches above.

The whirr of the nearby stone cutter jars my attention.
A basketball being dribbled says wop, wop, wop.
Car tires on the pavement and sounds of squeaky breaks float through the air.
Pencils and pens scratch on paper
As I write my thoughts and reflections down.

The world is full of things that seek to express themselves
Everything speaks its truth through the sound it makes.
Are humans the only creatures that try to disguise who they are?
What is my true and authentic voice

--Rose Lester

Starts and Stops

I sit
In silence that isn't silent.
And wait
for the voice in my head
        To stop.
A voice telling me:
        I'm not good enough
        No one will love the real me
        I'm bad or wrong
        Or a million other things.
The voice that has collected reams of evidence
        As to why the aforementioned
            Is true
            Is fact.

I sit
        In silence
And wait
        Straining to hear a new voice
            Faint and hesitant at first
A kind and gentle voice that says:
        I am enough
        Worthwhile
        Good
        Loved and loveable.

I sit
        In silence
And wait
For the scales within me to be
        Ever more tipped and weighted toward
Self-Compassion
And Grace

--Rose Lester

In Forest Deep

In forest deep wind and rain create symphonies.
On rocks, trees, and streams soft rhythms play.
A whispering wind over leaves, like a brush on timpany,
Spilling a pattering of drops in counterpoint to wind's melody.
A song, hushed like a lullaby, in beautiful harmony.

When storms gather, thunder rolls a deep voice out
Across the sky with lightning flashes sounding a crackling boom.
Rain streams down pounding out an angry beat,
On blade, tree and earth new sounds of rushing water.
Waterfalls rage like crashing symbols and kettledrums.

Water streams forth roaring, crashing, deafening.
Wind howls whips down valleys with a banshee scream.
Trees bend and bow away from the wind creaking.
Branches sway and tremble refusing to break.
Oak, Ash and Aspen, in concert their roots breathe lifting earth.

As the rain recedes, the crescendo fades.
Softly playing tap, tap, tapping in time.
Quiet restored bringing new sounds,
Birds sing and frogs call, while bees buzz
In sync with flowers under warm golden rays.

--Diane Lobre

Ocean Blue

On ocean's shore, waves bubble like champagne
Effervescently washing up onto silty sand
A backdrop to waves crashing like a bass drum
On rocks the crescendo of cymbals splash

A gentle lapping of waves playfully tossing pebbles
Upon receding as foam covers sand and shell a gentle shush
Swishing sand pulls back smoothing away tracks of man
A calm as tide recedes and ocean's gifts revealed

Swells pull deep building waves to immense power
Rollers tumble and crash against each other
At sea, dark clouds form, Thor's hammer strikes
Thunder and lightning stir the depths raging troughs

Pounding surf and turbulent waters sounding against cliffsides
Spray reaching to the sky, leaving a coat of salt and sea
Spouts form and twirl in a water dervish careening here and there
Energy released subsiding again in a oneness with ocean deep

--Diane Lobre

G(r)o(w)ing Up

Sitting, cross-legged, an abyss inside my mind
My head swirling with cerulean shadows
Fears and doubts banging against the shutters
BANG! BANG! BANG!
I don't whimper, I don't cry
I've grown tired of this disturbing charade.
Always… always, hating how I find myself back in this hurricane
All the negativity scratching like nails on a chalkboard,
GET OUT GET OUT! GET OOOOOUT!
I HATE BEING LIKE THIS!
But isn't this normal?
Everyone falls down, some of us farther than others
All there's left to do is climb back out
But what's the matter Vashti?
This isn't your first rodeo?
Why are you letting the white noise take over?
Why are you giving up?
Constantly having to revive myself…
It takes a hell of a lot out of me… and
…I don't want to feel this crummy anymore.

Yet, I'd hate myself even more for letting my demons win
They're laughing at me; they sound no different than those who say I won't
ever be good enough
That I will never reach up high enough
I feel the rage bubbling up in turmoil
I grab that rope and give it a vicious tug
Watch me; I'm going to reach the sky

--Vashti Lopez

Iridescent

Green echoes the thud of a rotting driftwood
hitting against an algae-infested riverbank
Orange reminds me of treasured warmth and winter
Brown tastes like spoiled apples and cinnamon

I want to go home to nights filled
with cerulean swirls and scintillating creativity
I miss the boiling yellows of a happiness
I can't seem to capture

Nonsensical blues and purples shade my voice
White noise fills my vision with crimson anxiety
Silver weighs down fluorescent lungs; I can't help smiling
It's beautiful yet hard to be alive

--Vashti Lopez

Stealth

It begins with the baby
fallen asleep at the breast,
after you detach the nipple, slipping
a finger to break the grip of toothless gums.
Leaving the white noise machine humming,
the door open a crack to hear her cry.

Everyone who ever mothered
or fathered or paid or took currency
or bartered to watch a baby knows:
should any sound wake her,
she will need your arms to lift
her up, your hands to cut the fruit,
your eyes to look out for the harm
she stumbles toward, eager,
and brings to her mouth.

The silence in the house: the same
your father imposed when you were his charge,
when he was not to be disturbed
in the living room by clink of knife
in jelly jar, by clank of dishes.
When a dropped glass would shatter the day.

Surface cannot help striking sound
from surface unless—it's longing,
a touch so light it can't be felt. He wanted
you to sit and read like him, alone
or with him, in the silence
in which he came back
to himself, back to the window
on the small fenced porch.

The taller you grew, the less he appeared
to hope he might do something with
the silence. Did he ever decide it was all
he wanted—not to slip away
from you too soon?

--Marit MacArthur

The Sound of Creation

The crinkle of paper skins of garlic
Being crushed by the weighty knife.
The chop, chop, chop of the cleaver
Dividing up the chicken,
Separating flesh from bone.
The sizzle of the olive oil
Spreading in the cast-iron skillet,
Smoking, exploding
When the diced onion is thrown in.
The swirling, swirling
As the wooden spoon stirs in the chicken.
The scrape, scrape, scrape
Of the spatula releasing the carmelized morsels,
The succulent suction
As the knife pops the seeds out of the lemon.
The splash and eruption
When the lemon juice is squeezed into the pan.
The cavernous hollow rumbling
Deep within one's belly.
The rush of salivation
Anticipating the feast.
The sensory overload
As the first bite fills the mouth.
Nostrils flare,
Tongue tickles,
Throat gulps.
The pleasure courses through the veins,
Spreading from stomach
to fingertips and toes,
Like lava
Replenishing the earth.

--Carla Martin

To Bring One Home

Do you hear it?
The plaintive drone,
A wild melody,
Drifting on the wind.

Follow me
Down cobbled alleyways,
Past stonewalled cottages,
Into fields of heather
Across a grassy moor.

The call is louder now,
Pulling you inexorably,
Stirring the blood
With cries of warriors
Marching into battle,
Fearing death,
Yet going forward anyway.

Your heart is filled with longing.
The wind is cold,
Making the reddened nose run
And eyes tear.
The sun is setting its golden blessing
Across the hills.
Serpentine stone walls cast shadows.
Sheep bleat,
Adding grace notes
To the haunting tune.

Stumble over a rise
And there they are!
Standing stock still
In rows upon rows,
Wrapped in crimson and emerald tartans
Whipping in the wind.

The highland pipers
Calling
At the end of day.

---Carla Martin

When My Mother Calls

As a child, playing in the park
or a friend's yard, my mother's
call turned me home before
she finished the second syllable
of my name.

Cars, girls, loud music - the thrill
of being young and loose in life
deafened me as she held fast
by the stove or the sink or the phone
screwed to the wall that never rang.

In later years, I'd remember the surety
of her voice. The way it rang out over
the neighborhood, clear and unmissable
like when I heard a church bell, distant
and faint, ring against my Sunday morning
hangover, lost in a stranger's sheets.

--Jerry D. Mathes II

What's There

The call of an elk startles me.
I look across the rolling brown
and gray hills at the sewing-machine
bobbing of pumpjacks
and feel the disappointment
shiver me like touching steel
on a hard frost morning.
It's the same feeling I get when
I mistake the wind cutting
through the wires for a whale's song
or the drivebelt slipping in a pulley
for the screeching laughter of little
girls playing who are gone.

--Jerry D. Mathes II

The Sound of Silence

Sound
A means of communication
A means of expression
Ears, hearing

Or none
A life changer
Different
Left out

Agonizing
Boring
Frustrating
Yearning

It's so hard to
Not understand
Misunderstand
Fail to communicate

I want
To know
It all
EVERYTHING

People talk
People laugh
People ramble
People mumble

I hate Not knowing
What has been said
What is being felt
What is being shared

I feel
Sad, angry
Empty
Alone

At times, though

It's a blessing
Political discourse
Can be exhausting

Distortions, lies
Not listening
To each other
Or even themselves

Turn off the TV
Skip social media
Take out my hearing aid
Check out for awhile

Sound
Life's connection
Or the lack of it
Silence

--Audra Miller

Shackled to Mistakes Made Again

Sirens wailing, they smell like regret, like the worst day of my life, and are as bright as what little future I might have left. Though my eyes are closed the blue red and white lights flicker. I'm unconscious, conscious. It's too late. Someone is banging on the glass. Seven hard long knocks and I'm awake. Window glass shatters as fast as the adrenaline coursing through my veins. I'm scared. My mind begins to race,

> How did I get here?
> What happened?
> Why can't I remember?
> Am I in trouble?
> What's going on?

My car door is torn open and I'm thrown to the floor. My hands are cuffed by a man in blue asking me what seems like a thousand questions. I can't focus. Everything is blurry my eyes are fixed. Fixed on a gold star pinned to the man in blue's uniform reflecting the lights from his car and keeping me in a trance. SNAP SNAP SNAP!

> "Sir, can you hear me?
> Sir, how many fingers am I holding up?
> Sir, are you okay?
> Sir, can you tell me how you got here?
> Sir, what's your name?"

A bright light clicks on as the man waives his flashlight from eye to eye. My name slides down the tip of my tongue and out my mouth. Two men in blue pull me up and one of them begins to speak, read, recite: You have the right to...

> I have rights,
> I have rights,
> I have rights,
> I have no rights,
> I gave them away.

I'm still hazy and I don't understand, but I don't resist. As I sit in the back of the car with the flashing lights that are no longer flickering and sirens no longer screaming, my mind is slow and I think to myself...

I got myself here.
I know what happened.
It's colorfully clear.
I'm in trouble.
I'm being detained.

How will I tell Nicole that I ended up here... Again.

--Mariah Morrow

Mission Moment

I was told
    close your eyes
I was told
    imagine five people
    imagine three women
    imagine two men
    imagine people you love dearly
I was told
    to mark three off my list
    to choose three to tell
    to choose two women to hear that
    to choose one man to hear that
They have cancer

I was told
    to tell three people I love
    to tell three people
               that they have cancer

I could not imagine it.
I have survivors in my family.
I have had people in my life die
               because of cancer.

I could not choose.
Could you choose?
Could you pick which loved one would hear those words?
I could not.
When I was told to imagine that,
      my eyes filled with tears
      my head shaking a silent no
      my voice voiceless
Because I could not face the truth-
          Two of three women
            AND
          One of two men
           WILL HEAR
         "You have cancer."

I imagine a day where I can
        tell cancer to screw itself
Because **no** men
Because **no** women
        will hear
        THOSE WORDS.

I want survival rates to be 100%
I want cancer diagnoses to be 0%
I want cancer gone
I want a world with more birthdays

Cancer can eff off and die.

--Samantha Nichols

Heels

Click. Click. Click.
Crimson heels on tile
Click-click, click-click,
click-click, click-click.
Faster pace for the woosh
and jostle of bodies.

The last one out,
crimson heels clicking confidently down the hall.
Knowledge descends on all.
Her confident stride heralding her arrival.

Click. Click. Click.
CLICK.
Crimson heels silently move in her sanctuary.
Expelling air,
she thunks her crimson heels and relaxes.

--Samantha Nichols

Sounding

Listen.
What do you hear?
A crashing cacophony
or
soft symphony?
Sounds everywhere,
inescapable, irreplaceable.

Rain falls on a metal roof, winds breeze through
birches, crickets trill sharply, boulders rock, roll
and rumble in a landslide tumble, creeks trickle
and gurgle, burros bray, babies cry, willows sigh,
ruby throated hummingbirds chirp, bumble bees
buzz, butterfly wings beat barely audible.
Thunder cracks. In the realm of the deep blue sea,
whales sounding sing songs of friendship, dare say
love, over fathomic distances afar.

Nature creates sounds with purpose, and mystery,
so vital nearly every creature and thing
on earth produces them.

Human utterances around ancestral fires
evolved to language and song, long before pen,
quill, stylus or hieroglyphics recorded
history and told our tales.

Words of poets resound mightily in crowded
coffeehouses. Politicians prattle and rattle
unruly crowds. Buskers play alone while
big bands boom. Lovers share secrets in near
silent whispers.

Sound existed here on earth before man, and
will be here as long as there is atmosphere.
May this be music to our ears.

--Christopher Nielsen

Accordion and Fiddle

Something about an accordion and a fiddle
maybe the way they meet in the middle.

Surrounded by all the others —
bass, drums, guitars,
hammered dulcimer.

Notes of heaven,
voices of angels.
From a Celtic country tune,
rhythm and folk blues
to a mariachi soul.
Magical musical poetry.

Something about
an accordion and a fiddle.

--Christopher Nielsen

Mama

Bones bounced between
your skin
clanging in hunger
Grinding against the cartilage of your
own
stubborn beliefs
As you bowed and bellowed against
any condemnation
awash with fervor

I offer
To wash your feet
An echoing: No
A resounding: No
and the peeling of skin
Scrapes and scaffolds
Like rungs on a latter no one
can reach, hollowness like a howling
wind as the cigarette tinges the nails
a little more yellow, the teeth, a little more
Yellow, your lungs, a little more gone,
Mama, a little more gone

As if to lullaby the child to sleep,
A plume of smoke crashes into wind chimes, wind pipes - like scattered glass

I can hear it Mama
An unwritten letter of goodbyes
Flipping, tossing, turning, page after page
But there's only airlessness now when
I hear you say, Mama

"It'll be alright."

--Chyna J Parker

Passerby of a Barking Rottweiler

You assume you're tough until
you walk past their territory.
Teeth and bark sharp,
unsure which was noticed first,
but no time to decide. The pounding four
feet of a blurred fur hurls itself towards
you. Your heart pounding to the same
rattle of the chain-linked fence—
the only net protecting you
when you are not the owner of a
Rottweiler. Remove your mask of
fortitude, for she is not fooled.
The erupting howl of Cerberus,
enough to break the strongest of heroes,
is a reminder of the fragility of life.
They stand their ground,
you hurry. An empty metal bowl
is hungry, but never full. You are
full of bones. If you aren't running,
you should.

--Marc Perez

Turn the Key

Turn the key, and hear the engine fail to turn over. Punch the steering wheel with face. An electrical issue surely. Release the hood, prop it open. Do everything in troubleshooting knowhow. Check the cables, wipe the battery clean, test the voltage, charge it anyway, jumpstart it. The click of the starter followed by stillness. Not even a sputter. Whack it with a wrench. Metal on metal. Turn the key with grimed hands. Still nothing. Watch it idle. The silence screams nothingness, which is what you'll be doing today. The dinging of the open door is mocking. Sit in the still car, a place where one becomes suddenly inclined to search mechanic DIY videos. Contemplate your own capability. Consider towing the car, getting it diagnosed, buying the part, paying for labor, picking it up. The silence is maddening. Turn the key. Turn the key. Turn it. Let out a scream, throw your keys. Retrieve them from the road. Go back inside and do it again tomorrow.

--Marc Perez

Mixtape for Mourning

Lyrics:

Is it okay not to miss you?
Can I reach out to our living mutual friends?
Should I offer my condolences to loved ones,
Even though they are better off?
Who should the drawings go to,
That I've stored away for years?
When you deleted all the pictures from your art Instagram,
Did anyone closer think to reach out to you?
Did they all feel, as I felt,
That it wasn't their place?
Is it okay not to miss you? x8

Tracklist:

Track 01: "Whiskey, Crying, Laughing" by Labi Siffre

Track 02: "Everything Sounds Like D-Flat Major" by Duke Ellington

Track 03: "Learning to Be Alone" by Tom Waits

Track 04: "Pouring One Out for the Homie" by Bob Dylan

Track 05: "A Brief Intermission with More Whiskey & Only Crying" by Elliott Smith

Track 06: "Insert Self Destructive Activity of Your Choice Here" by Joy Division

Track 07: "40oz of You" by Joni Mitchell

Track 08: "A Quick Interlude for Karaoke at the Dive Bar with My Superficial Friends" by Taylor Swift

Track 09: "Dabbling in Fleeting Delectation" by Outkast

Track 10: "Sweating Away the Memory" by Morrissey

Track 11: "Shave Your Head & Stand in the Rain" by Sinead O'Connor

Track 12: "Asking Inanimate Objects for Life Advice" by Simon & Garfunkel

Track 13: "Solace in Sex" by Frank Ocean

Track 14: "The Groovy World Graces Me with Her Harmony & Peace for Five Seconds" by George Harrison

Track 15: "Dealing with the Fact that I Never Knew You" by R.E.M.

Liner Notes:

Reading aloud to you,
Under a California ash,
Is where I'll find your memory.

The last few pages of Anne Frank's diary,
You could have given me hell for that,
You never did.

--Shelby Pinkham

Too One Tea One

Engraved Melody Slips the mind
Roaring unsaid rules stuck on *bar road* time
Mimicking screams fade within heartbeats
Confused *free dumb* translated by whispers
Expired emotions hidden beneath her breathes
Blocked opportunities *vibe rate* through the walls
Exposed excuses and puzzle *pea says*.

--Nashwa Rafiq

Left Unsaid/Muffled

All the things I have left unsaid
Would fill a book,
My hesitation
Another paragraph,
Every muted whisper
Another chapter,
And my confidence
Much too fractured,
Broken,
To speak another word.
Unearth
This coveted book,
In its torn pages
Covered in sounds of expression
Sounds of opinion.
Sounds of a voice.

Page one....
I wish I would have.
Page two....
If only I could have.
Page three....
I regret that I didn't.
Everything 'I wished'
Was always left unsaid.
Every 'if only'
Was the silent blur
As the storm quietly crept,
Every regret
Was the rustle in the wind,
As the storm fearlessly swept,
Everything else
Was the unrestrained rainfall
As the storm tamed its wrath,
And everything more

Is where I wept,
where my soul never slept,
Never rested,
Never dreamed.
Never spoke.
Repression has requested
My book,
But I'm reluctant to
Release
My silent storm,
My voice of
f u r y.

--Diana Ramirez

Verbalize/Vocalize

Hey you socially driven,
always charming,
words flowing,
spell binding,
crack a joke,
likeable
person.
I hate you.
You are one syllable away from enchanting the crowd,
And I'm struggling to pronounce a damn vowel,
You see,
"I" isn't in my vocabulary,
"I" dares not to be heard,
"I" cannot learn to speak up,
It must be a mute.
I don't wish it to speak.
But I wish it to crawl out of me,
Shed
And send
my body to the grave
Rise like a spirit,
Sing "I" into a song,
Make it a choir,
Speak "I" into a sound,
Make it the beginning of a
Fucking complete sentence,
Quite frankly,
I wish I knew how to introduce myself.
Introduce my vowel to the consonants,
Make them words,
Verbs to assert,
Spit flying,
Bold,
Swords,
Slicing into your conversation,

Not request a may before the "I"
Just state it.
I am here
And
I will remain.
And it's not you that I hate,
It's me.
I hate the lifeless mime I have become,
Imprisoned in my own box,
Thoughts taught
To become a fog,
And I'm a mortal ghost
Floating through the air,
An oxymoron,
And I've been cancelled out.
A smothered sound
And I didn t realize it was my hand
Over my mouth.
Excuse me
As I clear my throat,
Let me try this again,
Hey you socially driven,
always charming,
words flowing,
spell binding,
crack a joke,
likeable
person.
I am Diana,
Friendly,
Laugh at jokes,
Mind over matter magical,
Scatter brain,
Thinking too hard on what to say,
Frowning my way into bitch face,
In which case,
Enough said,
The social scene is beyond me,

I think it's time I go home.

--Diana Ramirez

Open Mic

It's another damp and amber Tuesday evening, which means that I am wondering if I should go to the show tonight, the show I went to last Tuesday, and the Tuesday before, and I smell the sticky, beer drenched floor, and I feel the creaks of the uneven, ripped-rug stage, imagining this time I will fall through to a swamp be stuck, upside down, face first in a mud pile, as my heart quickens its pace, thundering, as I contemplate the risk of embarrassing myself in a dungeon of comedians, modern court jesters and their friends, and maybe even the rare aficionado of the art, who may reject my attempt at five minutes of authentic connection, like a red balloon I blow up, hoping to burst it with my punch lines, but my other half reminds me that I owe it to my soul to stand-up, pay my dues, knowing that, at least for me, there is no other way to get to the land of large meadows with bright and shiny, rose-smelling rooms, filled with jubilant fellow humans, showering me with laughs, while I share and bare my soul to them, using silly words that ring in their ears and tickle their souls, and like last Tuesday, and the Tuesday before, I decide, YES, I must go!

--Michael Repik

I, Silence

You listen to me like
    a robin hears the worm.

She cringes at him when
    he scrapes the plate
        riling the wolf.

We breathe it in,
    we breath it out.

You avoid me like
    a sink full,

And when they find me,
    they finally feel alive.

--Michael Repik

The Silence Is Deafening

They say silence is the absence of sound
No birds tweet
No people speak
Nothing makes a sound
But that is not silence.

They say silence is when all is quiet
The breeze whispers without a voice
The band ceases to play
The air itself is still – no breath to be heard
But that is not silence.

Birds sing beautiful melodies
The wind whistling with them
People humming along
But there is something missing…

Trumpets blare and guitars riff
Viols sing in tune as drums keep time
A magnificent harmonizing affair
But there is something missing…

The voice I long to hear
The voice I cannot find
The voice that no longer speaks
This silence is deafening.

--Bailey Russell

Speaking with No Voice

Speaking with no voice
I heard my mother whisper
The words were strained and tense
Squeaking here and there.

Speaking with no voice
I heard the wind whisper
The words were light and airy
Swirling through the air.

Speaking with no voice
I heard the piano speak
The words were bright and cheerful
Lilting high and low.

Speaking with no voice
I heard a child speak
The words woven by her hands
Sharing what was in her heart.

--Bailey Russell

Boom!

BOOOOOOM!...
BOOOOOOOOOM!...
BOOOOOOOOOOOOM!...
POP! POPPP! POPPPPPP!
Shake and shudder
Rumble and thunder
Reverberations echo in my mind.
Reverberation echoes...
And echoes...
And echoes...
Loud clanks and clutters
Soft shhhhes and hisses
Leaking gas?
Leaking steam?
Whimpers and hooowwls.
Clattering. Scratching. Crunching. Crashing.
Contradictions abound.
Confusion. Fright.
More echoes in the night.
Go away!... Run!... Flee the fright!
Make it stop! Stoppp! Stoppppp! This scary night.
Not my New Year's Eve.

--Caroline Russell

Music, Melodious Secrets

Soft. Sweet. Serenely deep.
Some kind of treat?

Warmly embraced, comfortingly held.
Music transports the soul to places beyond sight.
Melodies stir memories:
fresh and old,
smiles and tears,
sometimes frightful fears.
Accompanied by words unfurls more tonal slurs
In the mind, in the soul.
Music...Replenish. Freshen. Restore. Renew...Faith blooms
Images abound from sound heard in our hearts.
We become more...blooming our souls as sound envelopes our core.
Vibration. Reverberation. Exaltation.

Soft. Sweet. Serenely deep.
Some kind of treat.

--Caroline Russell

Gold Is Rare

Silence is golden,
But gold is rare.
Certainly not quiet,
Noises are everywhere:
The tinkling of bells,
Footsteps that patter,
Endless droning behind,
Birds in the air.

--Sidney Russell

The Voice

Low and deep,
Strong and sweet,
Rumbling, softly,
Who is speaking?
The voice from my dream:

My child, you are chosen
Loved even as you are broken
Return home to hear
The choir singing
Merrily ringing –
Bells are tinkling.
Are you listening?

Low and deep,
Strong and sweet,
Rumbling, softly,
I am who am:
The voice from your dream

--Sidney Russell

Broken

All my expectations, high hopes and dreams,
seem to have faded
and withered away, with the
harsh blowing wind swallowing everything in its path.

The impact of such hit breaking my every belief,
almost like the sound of shattering glass,
as it hits the floor, every desire and aspiration vanished
as the sound of glass slowly, rapidly faded in the distance.

All my expectations, high hopes and dreams,
now gone with the sound of shattering glass,
can no longer be pieced together,
faded, then gone.

Fragments so fragile,
need special care,
for every shard of glass represents the whole,
a missing piece, an incomplete soul.

--Jennifer Samano

Mphondorho, a lion spirit

_Freed
__lion
___spirit of
____mphondorho
_____a baobob tree
_____Mozambique, how she glows.
_____"Aphani Wense," he shrieks,
_____"kill them all," a thunderous beat
_____a clamping shut of steel jawed gin traps.
_____Safe in Gorongosa, thunderous roar.

--B. Jordan Schmoll

Sounds of Home

So, my mother reminded me that they really did have to clean the tar off their heels after picking tobacco every thick wet August summer. Her brother Frank fed her bag a bit from his since momma had to make her quota or risk not getting paid and not having enough money to buy books for school. Cause as James Baldwin said, it's extremely expensive to be poor. But the point is, my mother's best friend Imogene surely did meet her husband in a debtor's prison bar. But that's another story. They grew up in the ankle of the Smokies and sometimes borrowed Frank's old car to drive to Greensboro. And Genevieve, the youngest, she gonna interrupt me in a minute to say no, the truth is, Imogene met her husband on the lawn during the tent revival, ya'll know which one. Genevieve has gone and educated herself so that she can teach that Shakespeare class at the Free Will Baptist Bible College in Nashville, Tennessee, and she can turn to that tardy student and in her learn-ed Cumberland syrup sway, say, "boy, have you eaten of the insane root that takes the reason prisoner?"

But it's Aunt Muriel who always calls at the right time. "Haaa darling, haa are you?" That's the life-giving drawl. "Breyet, did ya'll send me them flars?" And of course she means flowers but I never have the heart to tell her she speaks funny. Cause Aunt Muriel always says it right. "I'm so mayad I could eat a nail," she says with so much gumption but so little malice. And the family did keep that ol bus down by the Neuse River shore, and stands to reason something funny transpired down there, all them uncles and cousins and nine children and all. I'm shocked when Aunt Muriel breaks from her regional charm and dons the Scottish lilt of our ancestors as she recites that famous old Scottish poem:

> Have I ten storms left to see
> Or is this storm the last for me?
> How many scowls will this face abide
> Until I've scowled my last and died?
> And could I count on a single hand
> The sins left to commit for man?
> If I knew I had but one cup to drink
> Might I lay it up a while to think?
>> I think not, said the spider to the fly
>> All you've left to do is die.

And so when my mother rustles through my things after I was gone and cracks open my dog eared copy of Joan Scott's *Gender, a Useful Category of Analysis* and says to me, "Brett, I say, Brett are you a feminist?" Her drawl so dripping with Smithfield, North Carolina molasses that the ol neighborhood rooster, "Beau, I say Beauregard," stops dead in his tracks. But momma don stop there. And after becoming an American Baptist minister she confesses, "Brett, I think God might want me to be a feminist too." And her brainy memorial wilderness I continue to navigate across grass green shores. For her heart's a thousand colors but they're all shades of blue.

--B. Jordan Schmoll

Up the Stairway

I hear you racing, heart racing
As you take charge, in record time, to come say hello
"Good morning!" "Let's eat!" I translate
Your tone warps the more impatient you become

Each day it's like a drumroll, but the winner is self-evident
I favor calling it a draw

You win because you get to run around
I win because I can provoke the rumble
It's like peaches falling on the ground, but less bruised
Even if you do, you're resilient

How do I know?
I heard you race back up.

--Sa'miah Shakir

To Know Knowledge

Intellectual clamor is customary;
I was brought into the world, crying to know more,
But then I listened.
I listened to the silence, listened to myself listening.
I carved a cavity into the intellect with a nomadic tongue
And I made Knowledge speak.

So Knowledge spoke.
Its voice knew no barrier, nor did it know boundaries.
I heard nothing but Knowledge.
That clamor continued in my head,
Clinking, words cross hatching off the walls.

I had become a rattle.
I rattled until no wandering lexical wads could fit,
Only to have a constant dust storm
     whispering
The words and wonders I thought I knew.
I learned one thing at least.

--Sa'miah Shakir

The Sea-Scape

The year is 1943, Dong, dong, dong. The church bells ring, the bars are ice cold and frozen. I hear screams and then silence yelling that echoes through the halls, surrounded by endless darkness my only contact with the outside world are the church bells. Always on time and never late. The sounds of Keys begin to slowly fade away further and further away. But the bells ring on time regardless of my conviction. A storm is coming, and I pray it destroys this prison. I gaze at the seascape, the waters going in the direction the wind tell them to go. The cruelty of this place is sincerely dire. I hope it burns in a never-ending fire. All these things are incomparable to the pain I feel, the pain of thousands imprisonment here. If hell truly exists, I would say this is probably the place. What is this place? That is entirely up to you. Is it a real place ? Or a dark place of the subconscious ? To that... It's an enigma I longer know the answer to anymore. All I know is that the church bells ring as we near closer to midnight.

--Myles C. Shell

The Sound

It's loud
Never ending
A constant reminder
Of everything I
Can't hear
The sound waves
Reach my ears
While I'm trying
To ignore

It's screeching
High pitched
And angry
A constant alarm
That the waves
Will come
Whether I
Want them to
Or not

It's deafening
Drowning out
The sounds
Of everything
That could
Save me from
Despair

It's silent
Only perceptible
By those
Who don't want
To hear it

--Lena Smallwood

Coming and going

Less than an hour before first light
an owl murmurs under its breath,
only half awake. Like me.

Almost every morning
we pass each other—two itinerants
crossing the border of sleep.

--Don Thompson

Along the slough

Yokuts were no easier to find out here
than their ghosts are now.
An unobtrusive color, they blended in.
Their talk tended toward silence.

Women filled their baskets half-full,
then slipped back into the Tule reeds.
I hear insects not far off that could be
mortars and pestles grinding acorns.

Sometimes a jack rabbit will hold still,
testing the air. The hunter he scents
has been dead for a hundred years,
but the rabbit runs anyway.

--Don Thompson

Detention Room

A slowly drawn-out exhale
They want silence.

An occasional gust of
Hot summer wind runs up
And rattles the windows.
The faint, prolonged drone of
A lawn-mower travels into the room.

The low hum from the air vent
Fails to cool us off.
The gears in the clock
Chick, chick, chick.
They wish for silence.

His long black hair rustles
Against his windbreaker as he
Shifts in the small squeaky chair.
A soft whistle escapes
Through a breach in his left nostril.

Sticks slide amongst each other
In a muffled manner
In a small cardboard container.
A flame *chicks* to life.
A slow inhale.

The cigarette end crackles.
They demand silence.

--Donna Valdivia

House Party Aftermath

A sharp *tick* breaks the silence.
Metal clinks against metal.
The expanded wood slides
Against the frame. I made it
Home all alone.

My bare feet tap and unstick
From the cold wood floor.
My heartbeat is in my ears.
It's in the kitchen now.
It's in the living room.
It's pounding in the ears
Of all the dreamers.

They know, they know, they know.
Do they though?

Their steady and lulling breaths
Rise and fall in a breathy hum.
The sick one, the one who is sick
Whistles and wheezes
Above the rest.

My intruding heart fills the room
Fluttering and flapping frantically.
I want to make it stop.
I must make it stop.

They'll hear! They'll hear!
Do they know I'm here?

It's a hot night tonight.
Hot air tumbles in gently
Through the window spring
And ruffles the halo of hair
Of all the dreamers.

My heart is slowing,
An occasional muffled knock
In the cage of my chest.
The ceiling cracks and snaps

It was the ceiling. It was the ceiling.
Right?

I know. I know.
I am a permanent dreamer.

--Donna Valdivia

Café Symphony

Ding!! the bell echoes,
as customers' shuffle in.
"Welcome" waiters sing,
as guests acknowledge with grins.
Screeching chairs against the
crystal porcelain tile, waltz in unison
through the twenty-four hours.
Silver coated brewers' buzz, as glistening
brown rivers swirl into the mug.
Long faces along the marble
mumble for their dose of
caffeine. Clash! foam beer mugs,
on the other side, where wanderers
swig their grim misfortunes. Ding! the
bell chimes and the symphony will commence again

--Fernando Valdivia

Lake Huron

Swish… Swish sky-blue waves outline your feet,
in sync with the whooshing cuddling breeze.
Faint Ha-ha-ha's flood your surroundings,
above, a surreal picture-perfect sunny sky.

Bang! The sun dissipates before your eyes,
without a moment's notice. Murky shadows cluster
and cry, echoes of the roaring sky. Drip… drip
tears beat upon your glasses, observing from afar,
the waves rattling along.

In retrospect, it's a normal day at the lake.

--Fernando Valdivia

May

"May I have a cigarette?"
His weary eyes, you could say, were not
Eclipsed. Not Yet.
The corona shone—blinding us both.
Almost.

The after-image lingered with me—
Of a boy, alone, beginning
A lifelong, jarring scream
Peeling paint off carefully painted
Fences, round guardedly constructed,
Tilted houses
With bright lights
Showering down
Righteous streets
Framing
A perfect horizon of dying sons.

I remember that smile he gave me, now,
In different glow—
Shining lambent my presumptuous definition
Of "linger,"
As he broke the filter,
Struck the match,
Silenced scream in lung,
And walked away.

The smoke lingers in the air.

--Dylan Vaughn

From *Fragments of an Autobiography*

The Language of Mosquitoes

Cornbread for eyes. That's what
my grandmother used to say when
chickens or cats or grandchildren
lined up to eat. *Cornbread for eyes.*

Granny—Nellie was her grown-up
name—could twist a chicken's
neck faster than you could sneeze
or ask her *Is that for dinner?* Her

home and her husband's, Gramps,
my father's father, in southwest
Texas, near the road, not far from
the drive-in theater, is now (after

Daddy's death we sold it) a used
car lot. We could see at night bright
flickerings from the drive-in. We sat
outside with binoculars, worshipping

the images, making up the dialogue
passing between the characters and
us. They spoke in foreign tongues.
We slept in a screened porch, lying

awake to the language of mosquitoes.

--Tim Vivian

Your Forgiveness: During the Final Days of Masada Peter Speaks

I don't know where you went. And
I don't believe the lies that others
are telling. But with each breath
I take I hear malnourished roosters

crowing. Lord, can you hear them?
They're speaking in tongues, some
of them yours, some of them Herod's,
the words that now have meaning.

You ask me a question. Yes, Lord,
they do still build crosses. I'm an
old man now. No, the stories about
my prophesying in Rome, then being

crucified upside down, are not true.
I'm now here at Masada; it's forty
years after you left us. The Sicarii
roast traitors over our open flames.

I know, I will die soon. The Romans
are building ramparts up to us. We've
each gone to where we will leap. Each
nightfall, after the Romans stop, our

leaders, Gabriel and Michael, and the
myriads of angels, work all night to
shovel away what Pilate's ghost is
still commandeering. But they fail.

Soon, the Roman soldiers will climb
over God's last fortifications, swords
in their hands. But we will not be
here: the plan, which all of us have

agreed to, is this: all the men, seed of
Moses, Abraham, Isaac, and Jacob, as
the Romans breach the walls of Adonai,
will jump over the precipice into a

martyr's death. The Maccabees await
us. Though afraid, I too will jump with
them. But, unlike the others, I will hold
the one kiss by Judas in the deepest folds

of your clothing. On my way down into
sanctified death, I will hold on to this
kiss. Before I hit the earth of God's hands,
I will ask, and ask again, your forgiveness.

--Tim Vivian

Notes
Masada is an ancient fortification in the Southern District of Israel situated on top of
an isolated rock plateau, akin to a mesa. It is located on the eastern edge of the
Judean Desert, overlooking the Dead Sea 20 km (12 mi) east of Arad. Herod the
Great built two palaces for himself on the mountain and fortified Masada between 37
and 31 BCE. According to Josephus, the siege of Masada by Roman troops at the end
of the First Jewish–Roman War ended in the mass suicide of 960 people, the Sicarii
rebels and their families who were hiding there.

Malnourished roosters/crowing: see Mt 26:34-35, 74-75.

The Sicarii were a splinter group of the Jewish Zealots who, in the decades preceding
Jerusalem's destruction in 70 CE, violently opposed the Roman occupation of Judea
and attempted to expel them and their sympathizers from the area. The Sicarii carried
sicae or small daggers, concealed in their cloaks. At public gatherings, they pulled out
these daggers to attack Romans and Israelite Roman sympathizers alike, blending into
the crowd after the deed to escape detection.

The one kiss by Judas: see Lk 22:48, where Jesus says to Judas, "Judas, is it with a kiss
that you are betraying the Son of Man?"

The Maccabees were a group of Jewish rebel warriors who in the 2nd century BCE
took control of Judea, which at the time was part of the Seleucid Empire. After the
victory, the Maccabees entered Jerusalem in triumph and ritually cleansed the Temple,
reestablishing traditional Jewish worship there and installing Jonathan Maccabee as
high priest. The Jewish festival of Hanukkah celebrates the re-dedication of the
Temple following Judah Maccabee's victory over the Seleucids. According to
Rabbinic tradition, the victorious Maccabees could find only a small jug of oil that
had remained uncontaminated by virtue of a seal and, although it contained only
enough oil to sustain the Menorah for one day, it miraculously lasted for eight days,
by which time they could procure further oil.

Whispering

To the left, a harsh shushing, full of reprimand.
So loud, she's almost yelling,
With waving hands,
       Glaring eyes.
           Jabbing bony fingers,
                A deathly glare lingers.

    A Little Princess, 1888

              To the right, quiet mutters of solemn distress.
        Tearstained cheeks, sniffles, and whirling minds.
                    Can't make out
              The words,
         Of a mourning Mistress.

        Bath Consolidated School, 1927

      Middle brings a chaotic mess of adolescence,
      Giggling, goggling, and gossip.
      Bright eyes,
          White-toothed smiles,
             And lip gloss.

        - Sixteen Candles, 1984

--Michelle Whitaker

Thunder

when i was little,
sound of nature's power
rolling and trolling
into the dark of the zeus sky
ignited my primordial fear.

god's roar and warning,
doom in the distance,
encroaching in a coming
of a dark beast,
timeless, immortal
hades' shock wave.

now that i am grown,
from cloud to ground
lightning's conductor
plays the orchestra
of imposing pressure
built like a sorcerer's wand
magic boom draws to
low rumbling in the distance
lulling me to comforted sleep,
rain playing the strings of my windows,
reminding that all is renewed
and death has escaped me once more.

--Jana Lee Wong

Sounds of the Dust Bowl

loud "hee haw" out of an oklahoma scene
blisters on our heels from the river's bees
thrown in a jail cell for stealing some bread .
out of the orange groves, digging ditches dead,
playing guitar by river's bonfire light,
accordion background chimes in the night.

you don't know me
say you don't like me
hillbilly music
only thing that keeps me hangin' on.

buck owens' twang on a mosrite light,
pitter patter in the valley on fishing night
country coming from the studio street
down the corner from the barbecue's heat
knee slapping, twisting and dancing
loud amp with dwight yoakam -- broadcasting.

families still coming from out of the dust
hooting, hollering, as long as they must
snap of a jaw to the bakersfield sound
boys wrestling to the beat of those buckaroo hounds.
singing . . .
you don't know me
say you don't like me
how many of you that ever judged me
walked the streets of bakersfield?

--Jana Lee Wong

A Mean Piece of Water

"I'll never swim Kern River again."
--Merle Haggard

We perceive but frequency, flux
states that seem solid and static.

Behold the transmission of energy
through a medium, corn starch
in solution, river sand on steel plate.

Sound travels four times as fast
in water as it does in air.

The shape of the vibrating body
(*the shape of the cavity that contains breath*)
          determines the nodal pattern,

but the spectrum of the signal that excites the vibration

          determines which memory
resonates through all possible
permutations
                    to leave us haunted
by waves of successive compressions
and rarefactions,
                    of submerged
records rambling in fever
and silver wings the lung's limits.

As Merle Haggard sings, "I
can't hold myself in line."

--Matthew Woodman

The Fugitive

"I'd like to settle down, but they won't let me."
--Merle Haggard

Who wouldn't want to shed
their stripes in the shadow
of Mt. Shasta, the most
voluminous strato-
volcano astride the
Cascade Volcanic Arc?

Of the five essential
features of the phono-
graph, Edison opens
with captivity and
permanent retention
of all manner of sound-

waves previously stamped
"fugitive," reception
as a correlative
of regulation, San
Quentin California's
oldest prison and the

state's only death row. Escapes may be divided
into voluntary
or negligent, actual
or constructive, Haggard's
parole and then pardon

inexorably linked
to his band of Strangers
and the birdseye maple
Fender Telecaster
with the two-tone sun-
burst finish. To listen

is to risk being moved.
We are brief engagements
of time and pressure in
eruptive, ecstatic
song. Who wouldn't want to
be torn in a boxcar?

--Matthew Woodman

Effervescent

this selt
            zer sit
            s atop a sto
            ny seat beside
me it fizz
es   this sel
            tzer it fiz
zes
                    though e
ver   so   sli
                            ghtly
            sub
versive the way
this seltzer speaks to
            its seltzer self sub
tle this selt
                    zer its
                    sec
rets
            the seltzer's se
crets
                        accom
                            pan
                            ying
                the rain
            outs
ide

– Austin Yi

Jungles in the Dead of Night

        arrhythmical like   disease it slips
a limp
        in your step   and a
crook
        in your back
                luring lurid
                    wears upon
the nervous   system and produces   that
        feeling   we call
                            tired
        too much could cause
n e u r a s t h e n i a or an   or dep   xiety
                            ression or
                            head
aches or   fatigue etc
nervous   and   fidgety
perpetually   jerking   jaws
whatever   it's   doing
                it's   hazardous   its
        hot   sweat
                into   sweet
        tea—
      but the remedy for more   is more
unless interpreted by mainly paler pigments
to appeal to a wider commercial audience   so don't
with that inferior slush   don't forget about your country
              music
                and square dancing
                in public schools
                as weapons against
                jazz in the twenties

– Austin Yi

About the Authors

Sarah Alnagar is a sophomore English major, Film minor. Her specialty in writing, and favorite genre in general, is the world of horror; specifically, the world of slasher.

Shawn Anto is originally from Kerala, India. He studies at Cal State Bakersfield looking to receive his B.A. in English & Theatre. He was last seen on stage in *Dreamers: Aquí y Allá*. Past theatre credits include *The Profane*, "Gasoline", and *SubUrbia*. His writing has been featured or are forthcoming in *Reed Magazine, O:JA&L, Genre: Urban Arts, Mojave Heart Review*, and elsewhere. He currently lives in Bakersfield with his mini-rex rabbit, Elio.

Sherean Bledsoe is the Administrative Support Coordinator for the Department of Mathematics at California State University, Bakersfield, and working towards her undergraduate degree in Public Administration.

Greg C. Bolanos holds a B.A. in Theatre with a minor in English Literature from the California State University of Bakersfield (CSUB) and is incessantly pursuing a career as a director and writer. In and outside of The Film Club at CSUB (which he organized, lead, and whose members he mentored), Greg produced over thirty short films/promotional videos and continues to hone his artistic eye by generating original content. He is also a board member for *Project Oh Magazine*, an art collective based in Bakersfield. Greg recently relocated to Nevada to further advance his artisanal and occupational goals.

Jeremy Casabella teaches Composition and Literature throughout the San Joaquin Valley and writes poetry, short stories, and pwoermds. A 2019 Omnidawn Broadside Contest finalist, his poems appear most recently in *Vinyl, The American Journal of Poetry, GNU, Right Hand Pointing, The Invisible Bear*, and *Rabid Oak*. His pwoermding is featured in the anthology *The Wisdoms of the Universes in a Single String of Letters* from Xexoxial Editions, and on Twitter: @JCasabella1

Annis Cassells is a poet, blogger, teacher, life coach, and a member of Writers of Kern. Her work has been published in professional journals, hobbyist magazines, and local publications. She's had stories and poems published in online and print journals and magazines. This spring Annis published her first book of poems, *You Can't Have It All*.

Carla Chacon is a recent graduate of CSUB. She will begin her teaching credential studies in the fall. She plans to teach English at the high school level and hopefully help students find and develop their unique voice. Her writing has appeared in the literary journals *Drunk Monkeys*, *Rabid Oak*, and *Orpheus*.

Portia Choi devotes her time promoting poetry by hosting the monthly First Friday Open Mic and publicizing events during National Poetry Month in April. She administers **www.kernpoetry.com** with stories and pictures of poets and poetry events. She published a chapbook of her poems *Sungsook, Korean War Poems*. She is published in in *Orpheus*, *The Asian Pacific American Journal*, *KoreAm Journal*, *A Sharp Piece of Awesome*, *Primary Point*, *Writers of Kern Anthology*, *Emeritus Voices*, *Levan Humanities Review*, and *Invisible Memoirs*. She can be reached at ssportia@aol.com.

Taylor Clark is an English and Theatre double major at CSUB. She has been in several productions on the CSUB stage, including *Eccentricities of a Nightingale*, *The Importance of Being Earnest*, and, most recently, *The Dining Room*. She enjoys performing, writing, and taking pictures of her dogs.

When **Christopher Robert Craddock** isn't playing saxophone on stage at various establishments around town or debating with other members of the Hemlock Club at Dagny's, he blogs at https://chriscraddock.wordpress.com/

Nilsa Cubiascanas is a senior at CSUB who will start the teaching credential program in the Fall. Remember, a buttery drop biscuit recipe is always good idea to have in your pocket. The recipe, not the biscuit.

Yazmin De La Torre, an English major at CSUB, often sees the world as a cynical place, making it the best place to find inspiration to let the demons out, so this perspective is translated in both of her poems that show life isn't always cheerful.

When he isn't fishing obscure stretches of the Kern River, **Jeff Eagan** teaches English at Bakersfield College. He loves comics, David Bowie, and eating food that will probably kill him.

In her past life, **Valeria Espinoza** was a pirate infamous for her enthusiasm at forcing prisoners to walk the plank. She is currently serving her penance by crafting nautical-themed tattoos for indecisive drunken sailors. Check out her Etsy shop at https://www.etsy.com/shop/Cannera.

Is it destiny that **Shelley Evans** writes poems since she was named after Percy Bysshe Shelley, the English Romantic poet? Shelley Evans' verses have been published in anthologies, chapbooks, and online. Currently, she is finishing her first book, a poem written in memory of a beloved polar bear. Shelley is married, has three grown daughters and two dogs, and lives in Bakersfield working as a legal secretary. She is an active member of Writers of Kern, participates in open mic nights at Dagny's, is a member of the local Women of the Moose, and attends Parkside Church with her husband. The Kern County Library children's reading program, Barks and Books, was founded by Shelley and Marjorie, a black lab the Evans family puppy-raised for Guide Dogs for the Blind. Shelley is a beachcomber, sky gazer, and nature enthusiast who also enjoys swimming, wading, or just chillin' in any body of water! Walking on her "Longfellows" (big feet) through life with a positive attitude, joy in her heart, and a rhyme on her lips, she is ever-ready to let the light of God shine through her words.

Vickie Gage is currently a full-time college student living with her mother who is near the end of her life. She has three beautiful adult children and three grandchildren and a lot of emotional baggage that she has tried over and over to unload onto unsuspecting friends and family, and she has decided to try a new approach to healing with blogging, which you can follow at https://vickie.home.blog/

Tea connoisseur and sushi-serving extraordinaire, **Karissa Garcia** thoroughly enjoys all things artistic. A hopeless romantic at heart, Karissa spends her days eagerly searching for the next adventure. She sing-songs her way through life and is a firm believer that beauty can be found in unexpected places. Karissa thrives when drawing, singing, running, yoga-ing, eating, movie-watching, trying new things, and creating sick playlists on Spotify. She waits for the song to end before leaving the car and will call you when the moon looks especially beautiful.

Katie Gonzalez loves reading any work by Haruki Murakami. Currently majoring in English and a member of the Helen Hawk Honors program, she's a part-time swim coach and poet-in-progress.

Jason Grist is a CSUB alumnus with a bachelor's degree in English who has had his work published in Southern Oregon University's *OE Magazine*; U.C. Berkeley's *Ruah*; *Small Brushes*; *Orpheus Magazine*; *The Aurorean*, a poetic quarterly; *The Poet's Pen*; *Soul Fountain*, and various other literary magazines. His first collection of poetry, *Chasing Fall Colored Leaves*, was published in 2003. His second, *The Genesis of Fall*, was published in 2007. His latest effort, *In a Universe of Flowers*, can be found at www.bearstatebooks.com.

Jack Hernandez writes in cafes and coffee shops. His caffeine-inspired poems have appeared in journals like *A Sharp Piece of Awesome* and the *Anglican Theological Review*.

Monica Hinson is an English major currently attending Bakersfield College. In her spare time, she writes poetry and short stories. She has two dogs and enjoys hiking with her husband when they both have free time.

Anke Hodenpijl was conceived in Indonesia (Java to be more exact) just in time to escape the effects of being on the wrong side of the revolution, born in the Netherlands, survived the Great Flood of 1952 when the dikes broke, immigrated to the United States when she was five and was raised in Phoenix, Arizona. She is IndoDutch, a naturalized U.S. citizen and the youngest child of four. Her family history informs much of her poetry.

Catherine Abbey Hodges's most recent collection of poems is *Raft of Days*. Her first full-length collection, *Instead of Sadness*, won the 2015 Barry Spacks Poetry Prize from *Gunpowder Press*. Her poems have been featured on The Writer's Almanac and Verse Daily and nominated for Pushcarts and Best of the Net. Catherine collaborates with her husband, cellist Rob Hodges, and was named 2017 faculty of the year at Porterville College.

Anthony Salvador Jauregui III is a CSUB alumnus in English and Theatre. His favorite phrases are "Can I have chipotle aioli on the side, please?" & "yes, and..." Anthony spends his time working to support his craft. He plans on moving to Los Angeles this fall to pursue comedy & sketch writing and hopefully prove to his college professors that being a jackass in class gets you places.

Kelsie Nicole Jones has lived all over the U.S. from Connecticut to California, with interests waning from soccer to poetry. Having gotten her A.A. in Applied Music at Bakersfield College, she now continues her education at the University of Nevada, Las Vegas as a Music Education major. Poetry has been a long-standing love for her, and she is excited to be published for the first time since she began this beautiful journey.

Quinn Kelly is a second-year student at CSUB majoring in English and Biology. He enjoys long walks on the beach, non-alcoholic punch, and being a very awkward height in-between average and short. His poems primarily deal with complicated issues seen through a child-like lens, aiming to bridge the gap between terrible adolescence and snooze-inducing adulthood. He plans to continue writing even through grad school, hoping to publish a children's novel before 23.

When not lifting heavy batteries for his day job, **David Kettler** enjoys writing poetry, authoring books, or building metal sculpture pieces. *One Smart Antelope, My Reasons in Rhyme* and *Heavy Metaling* are three of his books that are available on Amazon. He has been writing poetry since he was very young and still does when inspiration strikes.

A retired teacher, **Judy Kukuruza** is a blogger and the author of *One Body Many Souls*.

Mateo Lara enjoys cheap wine and bad horror movies when he isn't writing poetry or being a bad person while trying to be a good person. He believes life, in general, is work, so we're constantly busy one way or another for someone or something. His poems have appeared in *The New Engagement* and *Orpheus,* and he has published two poetry books--*Keta-Miha and Other Poems* and *La Futura Tuga*--and one chapbook--*X, Marks the Spot*--all available on Amazon.

Rose Lester is a Marriage Family Therapist in private practice. When not seeing clients, she loves all things creative and expresses herself in many different artistic mediums. Her poems have been published in several anthologies and online websites. She volunteers for the Art for Healing program at Mercy Hospital. She can be reached at rosemft@att.net

Diane Lobre moved back to Bakersfield from Hawaii in 2013. She is retired and spends her days pursuing creative outlets such as watercolor and writing. She loves exploring new artistic endeavors and learning.

Vashti Lopez is a stressed-out college student who likes to eat an unhealthy amount of sweets and Asian cuisine. She's finally pursing her passion of becoming a creative writer. She's a bit antisocial, but apparently not so much, since she's presenting her work to a bunch of people today.

Marit MacArthur is Professor of English at California State University, Bakersfield. She holds a B.A. in English and creative writing at Northwestern University, a Ph.D. in English from UC Davis, and a MFA from Warren Wilson College. Her poems hand translations from the Polish have appeared in *Southwest Review, Leveler, Front Porch, Jacket2, American Poetry Review, Watershed Review, World Literature Today, Verse, Zyzzyva, Peregrine,* the *Levan Humanities Review,* and *Airplane Reading.*

Carla Martin has lived in New York, Scotland, Pasadena and finally Bakersfield, California for the past thirty-three years. She can be found entertaining students of all ages in the classroom with her stories and guitar or sequestered at a back table in a coffee cafe, writing poetry. A frequent performer at Dagny's Open Mic Nights, Carla also interviews other poets and songwriters for the website KernPoetry.com and is an avid supporter of the creative arts in Bakersfield. She has published poems in Writers of Kern 2018 Anthology: *Reach for the Sky* and CSUB's *Flora and Fauna* 2018. Her website is carlajoypoetry.com.

Jerry D. Mathes II is a book critic for *Orion: People and Nature* and is the author of four books. Two are *Shipwrecks and Other Stories*, and a memoir, *Ahead of the Flaming Front: A Life on Fire*, about his experiences fighting wildfire throughout the American West, including four years on an elite helicopter rappel crew and ten years as a crew boss and an incident commander. He had to give it up to be a single-dad to two girls, so took a job in an oilfield north of Bakersfield.

Audra Miller is a retired high school and junior college teacher, a community volunteer, and a member of a group of writers honing their writing skills. As a young adult, she lost most of her hearing, and can communicate in American Sign Language as well as English. She enjoys writing poetry.

Mariah Morrow is a Biotechnology major and part of the Greek organization Nu Phi Chi.

Samantha Nichols is a Bakersfield native. Sounds from around the area have inspired her writing for years. She is a graduate of California State University Bakersfield with a bachelor's degree in English Language and Literature and a minor in Linguistics. She aspires to be a teacher and a published author someday.

Christopher Nielsen has resided in Bakersfield, California for forty-seven years. He is a photographer, writer, web designer and consultant. Traveling the many back roads of California has provided a wealth of inspiration, and he feels most at home out in nature. Since the death of his wife of over thirty years, poetry has become his primary form of written expression. He is currently working on a book of Photo-Poetry. Christopher has been the featured poet at Kern Poetry's Open Mic at Dagny's. His photography has appeared in *Barren Magazine* and *West Texas Literary Review*. Christopher is also the Visual Media Director for the online literary publication, *Barren Magazine*. Author website: chrisnielsenphotography.com

Chyna Parker is a master's student who admires the art of writing; she hopes to use her passion for poetry in her career as a Licensed Marriage and Family Therapist. Chyna has been published by *Hinchas de Poesia, Orpheus,* and *One Book, One Bakersfield, One Kern.*

Marc Perez is a senior majoring in English at CSUB, and when he isn't sleeping in and arriving late to class, he can be found dodging stray dogs and traversing the streets on his skateboards.

Shelby Pinkham is a current graduate student and teaching associate at CSU, Bakersfield. She is a published poet, freelance copy editor and content writer, and an editor for the small literary journal, *Rabid Oak.* Her poems appear in the poetry anthologies *Writing Work* and *Writing Flora, Writing Fauna,* as well as *The Sand Canyon Review.* She aspires to earn a PhD in literature and/or creative writing; in the meantime, she is planning her first conference reading of her critical writing and writing her master's thesis.

When **Nashwa Rafiq** isn't hard at work writing meaningful poems or expressing herself through art, she works as a Payment Services student assistant. A senior at CSUB, she is a Liberal Studies major with a minor in Art.

Being a mother is her motivation, community is her drive, and life is her inspiration. **Diana Ramirez** works for local non-profit Links for Life and is a Board member for the Arts Council of Kern. Her love of poetry inspired her to organize Words Come to Life--a poetry-inspired art event which blends visual art, poetry, spoken word, and music. This event/project aims to inspire community connections and empower Kern County youth and adults given a second chance at life. On her spare time, catch her parking cars for Alpha & Omega Valet, volunteering for CASA of Kern County, exploring BookHounds with her two adventurous boys, or admiring the clouds in the sky. Daydreaming has always been her strong suit.

Michael Repik is a former Marine-turned-doctor, but he still can't drive a stick shift. After years of dealing with sick people, he decided to put down the stethoscope and pick up the microphone. "Dr. Mike" performs stand-up comedy all over the place and has even been heckled out of a nursing home for making absolutely no one laugh. He has recently returned to college and is pursuing a second degree in English Literature at CSUB.

Bailey Russell aspires to become an author and pediatrician. She hopes to open a private practice with her twin sister, which will later be expanded into a quality care clinic for people in the community who struggle financially and could not otherwise afford quality medical care. Her hobbies include reading, writing, and singing, and she loves to meet new people. In addition to reading and writing, she can often be found studying, working at the Writing Resource Center, or spending time with her family. She intends to obtain a Ph.D. in English – either medieval literature or philology – prior to attending medical school for her M.D., and loves reading mythology and folklore. Recently, she and her sister Sidney have also started painting table-top game miniatures as well as crafting things like miniature feast tables. If you're interested in seeing what they make, you can visit their Etsy page: https://www.etsy.com/shop/TwinsMiniMagic?ref=seller-platform-mcnav

Caroline Russell, a Type 1 Diabetic since 1974, has lived in Kern County almost all her life. In her youth, she attended San Diego State University, studying Psychology, Journalism, and Photography as well as taking on the role of President of the Public Relations Student Society of America. She went on to earn her Teaching Credential at Chapman College in 1987 before leading a fulfilling career as an elementary school teacher and later the leader of a Children's Liturgy Program at St. John the Evangelist Parish in Wasco, CA. Still, she says she didn't know what life and true happiness were until she had her first child at the age of 29½. Her kids are now the focus of her life, and daughters Bailey and Sidney are her inspiration and joy. She loves being around people and being in nature, though her outings have been limited lately due to contracting and battling Valley Fever.

Sidney Russell is an aspiring pediatrician and author. In the future, she hopes to open a practice with her twin sister and eventually expand it into a quality care facility for people who cannot otherwise afford medical care. She enjoys reading, writing, and meeting new people. When not reading or writing, she is typically studying, working at the Writing Resource Center on campus, or spending time with her family. Before going on to pursue her M.D., she will work toward a Ph.D. in English – medieval literature or philology, and she is always on the prowl for a good mythology book. Recently, she and her sister Bailey have also started painting table-top game miniatures as well as crafting things like miniature feast tables. If you're interested in seeing what they make, you can visit their Etsy page: https://www.etsy.com/shop/TwinsMiniMagic?ref=seller-platform-mcnav

A first-generation college student on the road to becoming an English teacher at the high school level, **Jennifer Samano** uses the art of creative writing to help find her inner voice.

A historian by trade, **B. Jordan Schmoll** originates from the boiling foothills of Bakersfield. A fellow of the South Coast Writing Project (SCWriP), Schmoll's writing has appeared in a variety of publications, from the literary journals *Mojave Heart, Orpheus,* and *Rabid Oak* to the *Journal of Appalachian Studies* and the *Journal of Spanish Cultural Studies*. He teaches in San Luis Obispo and calls Santa Margarita, CA home.

Sa'miah Shakir is a sophomore English major student who plans to become a middle school teacher once she graduates. She is currently a member of California State University, Bakersfield's Film Club. As a writer, she is most interested in writing about selfhood and variables that mold the self. In her leisure, she enjoys creating her own writing and is currently learning the piano, Spanish, and Portuguese.

Myles C. Shell is a sophomore English major and Business Administration minor at Cal State Bakersfield with a passion for both art and poetry.

Lena Smallwood is a 16-year-old stressed-out high school student who enjoys dancing, singing, and acting. This is her first poem submitted to an anthology. She hopes to have more works in the future.

Don Thompson's most recent book is *Outdoor Chamber Music,* a collection of plein air poems. *Suite Pneuma* will appear this fall. Visit his website at www.don-e-thompson.com

Donna Valdivia is currently attending California State University of Bakersfield as a junior and is majoring in English. Prior to transferring to CSU Bakersfield, she attended Porterville College where her English professors encouraged her to stay on the path of becoming a wonderful instructor. Donna aspires to be an English professor at a community college in hopes of helping others succeed in their educational careers. During her free time, she enjoys looking after her four younger siblings, being outside around nature, and exercising. All three of these activities help her to remain a humble, attentive, and optimistic person.

From Grand Rapids, Michigan but currently residing in Bakersfield, California, **Fernando Valdivia** is a junior majoring in English at California State University, Bakersfield. An avid reader by day and an ambitious writer by night, he spends his leisure time playing the Ukulele or reading his favorite author Virginia Woolf.

Dylan Vaughn loves the Beats but hates social media and can be found at Lengthwise brainstorming ideas for future poems and stories.

Tim Vivian has published numerous books, articles, and book reviews in his academic field of study, early Christian monasticism. He has lately turned more attention to literary efforts, publishing articles on the poetry of Denise Levertov and Rowan Williams and on the novels of Marilynne Robinson. You may reach him at tvivian@csub.edu.

Michelle Whitaker is currently a sophomore studying Criminal Justice who hopes to become either a prosecutor or a profiler someday, and would like to use her retirement to open a horse and dog rescue. One fun fact about her is that she was once attacked in the face by a Red-Tailed hawk! Luckily, its claws just missed both her eyes and the scratches didn't scar.

Jana Lee Wong has poems appearing in *The Levan Humanities Review* and *The California Quarterly of Poetry* including "Letting Go," about the love for her daughter, "Soul Mate," a tribute to her husband, and "Time on Monk's Hill," about seeking truth and inspiration. By day, she teaches seventh and eighth graders at Standard Middle School, and by night, she teaches English at Bakersfield College. Her hobbies include traveling, swimming, hiking, cycling, and writing science fiction and poetry. She can be reached at jana.wong@bakersfieldcollege.edu.

Matthew Woodman teaches at California State University, Bakersfield and spends too much time worrying about foolishness. More of his writing can be found at www.matthewwoodman.com.

Austin Yi is easily moved by clichés. He spent most of his time in London watching tv at the hotel and eating cuisine he could easily find at home. Catch him on his bike.

Community Partners

Without like-minded friends and strangers, an artist would be little more than a voice in the wilderness, writing, creating, and reciting for an audience of stone and wind. Thankfully, we have those accomplices that keep us energized and connected.

Thank you to our literary community partners, who are making Bakersfield and Kern County more vibrant, more imaginative, more inclusive, more beautiful.

Wr.ters of Kern (WOK) is a branch of the California Writers Club (CWC). One of the nation's oldest professional clubs for writers, CWC was founded by Jack London and fellow writers in 1909 for the purpose of helping aspiring authors socialize with published authors.

The Writers of Kern is a non-profit organization bringing together professional writers and novice writers in a creative and supportive atmosphere. Published writers share their knowledge and skills through critique groups, at general meetings and during conferences and workshops, and non-published writers gain experience, encouragement, and guidance to help them become published writers. Meetings and critique groups are positive, uplifting events meant to inspire and motivate all writers to dedicate time to the fulfilling craft of writing.

For more information, visit writersofkern.com

FIRST FRIDAY Open Mic is held every First Friday at 6:00 p.m. at Dagny's Coffee in Downtown Bakersfield.

The sign-in for the free and public Open Mic is at Dagny's on the night of the event. On most evenings, there is a featured poet or a musician.

For more information, contact Portia at ssportia@aol.com

Sponsored by Dagny's Coffee and Kern Poetry

ART AFTER DARK

LAST THURSDAY
EVERY MONTH

1930 R ST
BAKERSFIELD, CA 93301

bmoa.org/artafterdark

Bakersfield Museum of Art

Recent Publications by Our Contributors

Every library needs to grow, to breathe, to expand. Help your bookshelf exercise its muscles by picking up a recent publication by one of our authors.

Poems that celebrate and remember.

Poems that observe and question.

Poems that honor life, love, and friendship.

In *You Can't Have It All*, Annis Cassells navigates the sometimes sparkling, sometimes treacherous waters of family, identity, migration, and politics and in the process shows us both how to hold on and how to let go.

SUNGSOOK

KOREAN WAR POEMS

PORTIA S. CHOI

As a young child, Portia Choi observed first-hand the horrors of the Korean War. In *Sungsook*, Choi writes honest, heartfelt poems that portray the courage and resilience of refugees struggling to survive, without sacrificing the charm of the little girl. Rich in sounds and images, the poems recall the terrors of war as well as the pleasures shared with a sister and loving mother. As an adult in California, having immigrated to Los Angeles at age eight, Choi now befriends Korean War veterans and tells their stories too. In this remarkably beautiful poetry, the author draws us into wartime as if we were experiencing it ourselves, step by step and mile by mile.

There is a brilliant subtlety to this witnessing, a knowing tenderness that explores our relationships with the natural world and those we love. These poems exalt the moment and explore the geography of memory, with a spare clarity that evokes our finest lyric poets' imaginations.

--Lee Herrick, author of *Gardening Secrets of the Dead*

In Catherine Abbey Hodges' second collection of poems, . . . the complexities of faith huddle close to the ordinary work of cooking, making lists, and keeping a steady breath. This is an authentic and beautiful book.

--Emma Trelles, author of *Tropicalia*

There is an important well of reflection as a human. Understanding there will always be sadness, but the future holds more than just that. It holds glory, it holds bliss, it holds power, and magic—far away from wars, blood, and the greatest sadness. It all comes with a lesson. Absorb. Adapt. With this collection of poetry, Mateo Lara aims to look at the self and the world around. To understand what sadness means, but also, what it could hold for the future, through love, friendship, loss, pain, and growth.

SHIPWRECKS
and Other Stories

JERRY D.
MATHES II

In *Shipwrecks and Other Stories,* we read of men and women struggling in love and longing, adultery and addiction, between staying in a place and moving on, while trying to rediscover who they are. We are abandoned with an exiled Guatemalan Special Forces Major and his family on the US-Mexico border when he discovers smugglers trafficking kidnapped girls and faces the decision to attempt to rescue the girls or ignore them and not risk his family's safety. We stand in a rainy night with a commercial fisherman, still reeling from an accident at sea, as he finds hope in the skeleton of a ship that will never float. A hunter tracks the mountains for a wounded elk as he comes to terms with economic changes and having to leave the place he grew up. Two women confront each other about the affairs they had with each other's husbands. In the Meadow Award winning novella, "Still Life," a paramedic spirals into the Las Vegas drug underworld after accidentally killing a girl, but still struggles to do something good. These and other characters haunt the fringes of their own lives shipwrecked in society as they seek identity, hoping to rescue themselves.

In *Outdoor Chamber Music,* Thompson has gathered a selection of plein air poems, written during a year in which he decided not to work at his desk at home in the farmhouse where his wife Chris' family has lived for four generations. Instead, he drove every morning to someplace nearby where he responded to the surrounding landscape: the Elk Hills, the California Aqueduct, canals, nut groves, horse ranches, and dairies, fields and fallow land. These poems are specific, noticing flora and fauna that is often overlooked, but they also resonate with something numinous.

Writing Fields

field \field\ (f[=e]ld), n. [OE. feld, fild, AS. feld; akin to D. veld, G. feld, Sw. f[aum]lt, Dan. felt, Icel. fold field of grass, AS. folde earth, land, ground, OS. folda.]

1. Cleared land; land suitable for tillage or pasture; cultivated ground; the open country.

2. A piece of land of considerable size; esp., a piece enclosed for tillage or pasture.

3. A place where a battle is fought; also, the battle itself.

4. An open space; an extent; an expanse. Esp.:
    (a) Any blank space or ground on which figures are drawn or projected.
    (b) The space covered by an optical instrument at one view; as, wide-field binoculars.

5. (Heraldry) The whole surface of an escutcheon; also, so much of it is shown unconcealed by the different bearings upon it. See Illust. of Fess, where the field is represented as gules (red), while the fess is argent (silver).

6. An unrestricted or favorable opportunity for action, operation, or achievement; province; room.

7. (Sports) An open, usually flat, piece of land on which a sports contest is played; a playing field; as, a football field; a baseball field.

8. Specifically: (Baseball) That part of the grounds reserved for the players that is outside of the diamond; -- called also outfield.

9. A geographic region (land or sea) that has some notable feature, activity or valuable resource; as, the diamond fields of South Africa; an oil field; a gold field; an ice field.

10. A facility having an airstrip where airplanes can take off and land; an airfield.

11. A collective term for all the competitors in any outdoor contest or trial, or for all except the favorites in the betting.

12. A branch of knowledge or sphere of activity; especially, a learned or professional discipline.

13. A location, usually outdoors, away from a studio or office or library or laboratory, where practical work is done or data is collected; as, anthropologists do much of their work in the field; the paleontologist is in the field collecting specimens.

14. (Physics) The influence of a physical object, such as an electrically charged body, which is capable of exerting force on objects at a distance; also, the region of space over which such an influence is effective; as, the earth's gravitational field; an electrical field; a magnetic field; a force field.

15. (Math.) A set of elements within which operations can be defined analogous to the operations of addition, subtraction, multiplication, and division on the real numbers; within such a set of elements addition and multiplication are commutative and associative and multiplication is distributive over addition and there are two elements 0 and 1; a commutative division ring; as, the set of all rational numbers is a field.

29651153R00095

Made in the USA
San Bernardino, CA
16 March 2019